Shades of the Sublime & Beautiful

John Kinsella is the author of over thirty books, and is editor of
the international literary journal *Salt*. A Fellow of Churchill College,
Cambridge University, he moves between the Western Australian
wheatbelt, the fens of Cambridgeshire, and the USA.

Also by John Kinsella

Poetry (includes)

THE FROZEN SEA
NIGHT PARROTS
THE BOOK OF TWO FACES
ESCHATOLOGIES
FULL FATHOM FIVE
SYZYGY
ERRATUM/FRAME(D)
THE SILO: A PASTORAL SYMPHONY
THE RADNOTI POEMS
THE UNDERTOW: NEW AND
  SELECTED POEMS
LIGHTNING TREE
GRAPHOLOGY
POEMS 1980–1994
THE HUNT
KANGAROO VIRUS
SHEEP DIP
ALTERITY: POEMS WITHOUT TOM
  RAWORTH
THE BENEFACTION
FENLAND PASTORALS
VISITANTS
COUNTER-PASTORALS
WHEATLANDS
ZONE
ZOO
THE HIERARCHY OF SHEEP
RIVERS (with Peter Porter and
  Sean O'Brien)
LIGHTING TREE
PERIPHERAL LIGHT: SELECTED
  AND NEW POEMS
DOPPLER EFFECT
THE NEW ARCADIA
LOVE SONNETS
AMERICA: A POEM
SACRÉ COEUR: A SALT TRAGEDY

Fiction

GENRE
GRAPPLING EROS
CONSPIRACIES (with Tracy Ryan)
POST-COLONIAL: A RÉCIT
  (forthcoming)
MORPHEUS: A PARADIGM
  (forthcoming)

Plays

DIVINATIONS: FOUR PLAYS

Non-Fiction (includes)

AUTO
FAST, LOOSE BEGINNINGS:
  A MEMOIR
DISCLOSED POETICS: BEYOND
  LANDSCAPE AND LYRICISM
CONTRARY RHETORIC

As Editor (includes)

LANDBRIDGE: AN ANTHOLOGY
  OF AUSTRALIAN POETRY
VANISHING POINTS:
  NEW MODERNIST POEMS
  (with Rod Mengham)
SCHOOL DAYS
PERSIAN WHISPERS AN
  ANTHOLOGY (with Ali Alizadeh)
THE NEW PENGUIN ANTHOLOGY
  OF AUSTRALIAN POETRY
  (forthcoming)

Shades of the Sublime

JOHN KINSELLA

& Beautiful

(come out of Edmund Burke's
*A Philosophical Enquiry into
the Origin of Our Ideas of
The Sublime and Beautiful
With Several Other Additions*)

PICADOR

First published 2008 by Picador
an imprint of Pan Macmillan Ltd
Pan Macmillan, 20 New Wharf Road, London N1 9RR
Basingstoke and Oxford
Associated companies throughout the world
www.panmacmillan.com

ISBN 978-0-330-45377-6

9 8 7 6 5 4 3 2 1

A CIP catalogue record for this book is available from
the British Library.

Printed and bound in Great Britain by
Mackays of Chatham plc, Chatham, Kent

Contents

PART I

Novelty, 3
Nyctalopia: pain and positive pleasure, 5
Joy and Grief, 7
Station Road: Sympathy, Imitation, and Ambition, 13
Sympathy – Bogged, 16
Of the Effects of Tragedy, 18
Imitation Spatialogue, 22
The Last of England, 27

PART II

Astonishment (Of the Passion Caused by the Sublime), 31
Terror, 33
Clearness, 34
Like Power, 35
Privation, 37
Vastness: A Glimpse of Alaska, 40
Journal (Vastness), 43
Lover's Leap, 44
A Difficult First Harvest. Wheat Variety: Carnamah, 48
Wave Motion Light Fixed and Finished, 52
Light: King of the Burnout Shows Full Range of Emotions, 56
Colours of the Wheatbelt, 57
Loudness, 58
Swoop (suddenness), 61
Intermitting, 63
Stench, 65

PART III

Proportion not the Cause of Beauty in Plants, 69
Proportion in Family Portrait in Regional Gallery, 70

Gradual Variation, 71
Beauty in Colour, 75
Deluge (cant) / The Eye, 76
Ugliness — A Vision, 78
ESP in the Wheatbelt, 80
Textures of the Wheatbelt, 81
Sounds of the Wheatbelt, 83
The Tastes of the Wheatbelt, 84
Smells of the Wheatbelt, 86
Clearing of Beauty, 87

PART IV

Association (Sublime/Beauty): I drove on, a ghost . . ., 93
Fear, 96
Riding the Cobra at the York Show (The Artificial Infinite), 97
Terrible Darkness (Against the Racism of the Sublime), 99
Concerning Smallness: Golden Whistler, 103
A Place of Lichen, 104

PART V

Some: an ode to the partitive article, 107
Station Road and The Common Effects of Poetry, Not by Raising
Ideas of Things, 109
Wet Wood, 111

AN ADDITION

Into the Sun, 115
Night Recall Station Road: typed in darkness, 117
Stone Flung Near Head of Observer, 119

A SECOND ADDITION

Forest Encomia of the South-West, 123

for Emily Apter

PART I

Novelty

Around the district occasional wedge-tailed eagles—
even, one afternoon, three, possibly four
on the sunset side of the mountain; yesterday
a first notarised—a massive wedge-tailed flying
from the mountain straight over the house, heading
south—the largest eagle I've seen, at least a ten-foot
wingspan, maybe fourteen, with a slow cruise
up the line of the gravel driveway, a rippling shadow
cast in multiple directions, as though the low winter sun
was just one of many hidden suns—it was, possibly,
a Roc—it scanned slowly from port to starboard,
surveying, though not predatorily. Its purpose
was not the assuaging of hunger, clearly.

Shortly before the appearance of the eagle,
walking the drive with my toddler Timothy,
we came across an owl pellet below the most distended
limb of a greyed dead York gum—the limb over the ochre
and stagnant waters of the driveway favoured by irrupting
birds—a perching place, a stopover between river and mountain:
black-shouldered kite, white-faced heron, egrets, cockatoos,
twenty-eights, magpies, crows—generally, larger birds.
At the exact point of passing over this event horizon
the eagle began its visual sweep, also, a Cessna was directly
above the eagle, though thousands of feet higher. It was
confluence and syzygy. The owl pellet on the ground below
suggests night birds perch in the dead tree branch also:
owls, tawny frogmouths, owlet nightjars. This was the pellet
of a large owl—a grey matting of skin and bone—a mouse—
and, strangely, a length of string wound like intestines
or an umbilical cord through the body waste. Ants were busy
divesting it. Ants have set up colonies at the drop zone.

It must be a semi-regular occurrence, one might hypothesise
from this. My toddler called the eagle a plane, and fixated
on the ants — slowing down with the encroachment of evening.

I am guessing it's a Boobook owl — I've often heard
the "boo-book" anagrams at night, and have seen them flutter
heavily at dusk down near the shed. The Roc has left stories
and exclamatory prose — we are still talking about it — solidly — today.

Nyctalopia: pain and positive pleasure

Ebblight, crepuscular revelation of negative space,
      what else can you do
          but discuss the light,
slightly charged bats that highlight
          against background filling out
all other space?
          Numbed by grammar,
      slippages are traduced,
        a removal of pain
as delightful as rashes
      of Paterson's curse
against the mountain's flanks,
          waves on dams tossed
after storm to decline in horror,
               spectators
on the ochre banks;
        but now the calm,
            a blank
pleasure in the solid object,
         wariness
of walking into a sharp corner,
      a blunt shin-chipping
outline,
        wandering or hesitating or blundering
hands out — clearlight flashback,
            hallucination
       saying all is upright
and in its rightful place
      in clarifying nightlight —
body dint and stint
        under Mary Shelley's
sun lamp intimating pain gone

                    as just relief
and little or no pleasure,
            given its other name,
terminology;
                    the grinding of wild oats,
hatching out of lupin pods, spring
            unable to kick into action
                    but still working hard at fruition,
        excessive growth
swaddles the trails,
                    places where feet will be torn
apart;
        lacking vocabulary in thickening dark,
Strindberg assails dramatic inaction —
                                    lighthouse
full to the gills, refugees, evacuees,
                        those 2500
handguns sold in Monroe, Louisiana
the day the homeless arrived from New Orleans,
shellshocked by the white
                    light of nation;
                                I can't see
the hurting, the deliciousness, obvious delight
            of media, stimulus
                    of the word 'terror'
        that blazons
like chemiluminescence
                    in the cursed purple flowers
showing only at night,
                        spiritualisms
of weed control,
                    tidal obstacles
        so lacking
in the light we refrain.

Joy and Grief

"The surprising thing about Corrigin is that the town's most unusual and interesting attraction seems to be passed over by the Tourist Information Office. About three or four kilometres out of town on the road to Quairading is a dog cemetery where loving owners have gone to the expense of having quite elaborate headstones placed over the remains of their faithful four legged companions. Thus very human looking gravestones are dedicated to 'Dusty', 'Rover' and 'Spot'. To find such a strange place outside an unassuming little wheatbelt town like Corrigin is both fascinating and bizarre. Is this the resting place of the local sheep dogs or is it restricted to pampered domestic pets?"

Sydney Morning Herald Travel

The firebreaks needed to be done and I've now got a sunburn so bad
my neck has turned red
    and peeled savagely,
        leaving me pained by hegemony
and consensus,
    participatory as the shire rangers cruise the district
searching out compliance;
        by way of distraction and relief,
            window
of the car open at max speed to cool the social bite ringing
my neck,
    a mass of distraction and confused role-play
as no one can pinpoint class origin or the myths
we throw up around ourselves,
        like Bookchin
from an urban affront taking on Ed Abbey's
disturbing "Defence of Rednecks",
by way
    of branching south-east

about sixty-nine kilometres
to Quairading
           and then another sixty or seventy to Corrigin,
greeted on the outskirts —
                     that is, still on the Quairading Road . . .
road for country folk . . .
                not the tourist run,
           not the pragmatics
of the two-and-a-half-hour drive
                on the Brookton Highway
from the City —
                But a Dog on a Ute — cut-out dog
on a used, abused, and now good-only-for-sculpture
utility vehicle,
           comical terror
           good-natured if perverse
           and parodying conceits
woven on the banks of a farm dam in a paddock
                already hay-cut
           in this slow Spring —
                          towards the town
famous
           for its Dog in a Ute muster,
                          world record 1527
dogs of all species in utility vehicles of all makes
in 2002,
           in its ongoing competition
                          with the Victorians
(Australian Rules is big there as here, as in Corrigin,
and if the term "redneck" finds its origin
with Scottish lowland Presbyterians
making their blood-writ red-rag-around-the-neck rejection
of the Church of England, dashing to Ulster and the North Americas,
so the Irish have something to do with it *here*,
despite the English-sounding names of landowners

and many of the workers . . .),

                        especially those of Warrnambool
who managed 797
        to hold the world record briefly,
this dogtown,
        dog at the wheel,
                hot-dogged
        rip-roarer,
        port and polished, chromed gnashers —

                          towards the famous
Dog Cemetery,
        "Man's Best Friend's" resting place,
        drive-in Ramones grief patch
                or double serve of irony
or both,
        to drag the sorrow out,
                    to pleasure our loss:
                              Stephen's
old working dog Shep
        never made it as a worker
        because of a crippled back leg,
the original owner
        wanting to shoot it
                straight after the accident . . .
                        in dog years,
he's 105 years and counting,
        and his loss one day will be a loss
equivalent to the loss
        of almost one of us, almost . . .
                  and out of the *bizarre*,
the redneckery of the dog cemetery,
                there'd be countless
cases,
        if some of perverse humour,
        misanthropy,

a way of getting back at the graves
        that can't be desecrated
                in a human cemetery
without serious prison sentences;
                        I don't know anyone in Corrigin,
and in reality
        it's an hour-and-a-half's drive from our place,
        and though also wheatbelt
                it's different wheatbelt,
and there's twisted angular Pythagorean gimlet trees
out there,
        which are not here;
                    but the town — despite its excellent
nature reserve surrounding the air strip,
and its sense of humour that some think might make it lucky,
an outpost or outrigger on the never-really-formed tourist circuit,
a town made late because it went nowhere really —
                            is still caught up
                  in the myth
of growth through poison,
        proud of its spray services,
           its spray rigs,
its abattoir,
French word
        as euphemism
        in the districts
of slaughter;
        and so, in my self-myth of belonging,
                      of a classless
participation in what I know best but remain alienated from,
that I can't leave,
        can't get away from,
        this inside-outside
paradox that draws me to the dog cemetery,
                that prevents me

nudging the car too far into the gravel entry —

a desire

to show respect to the dead,
> respect to those who come
to grieve over their dead,
> who joke over the names of the dead,
the quasi-human de-anthropomorphics,

allegorical

still lives and wastelands and distraction
to the passers-by
> who might laugh or celebrate, even aspire . . .

With his

prejudice against Shelley,
> I wonder what Eliot,
> > or say Leavis
with his "weak grasp upon the actual"
take on Shelley and his poetry,

might make

> of the Dog Cemetery,
> > of the joy it gives
the shearer or cocky who has lost a loved one,
> a loved dog,
a shearer or cocky whose neck is burnt in the sun,
> who is probably as racist or not
as Eliot or Leavis,

who drops in on the grave with mates

and has a beer,
> or, sometimes,
quietly alone,
> hearing cars approach,
standing bolt upright, kicking a stone as they rush past . . .

Corrigin,

Tidy Town,
> I ask your forgiveness,
> your indulgence,

your welcome,
and though I think your Loch Ness Monster on the town dam
looks barely absurd enough to warrant interest,
I ask you
   to give me a fair hearing,
   to let me go back across the wheatbelt
   to the town —
       oldest inland town —
            I can't escape,
where my neck grows malignly red clearing the firebreaks,
where Shep hangs out
      keeping his eye on the action:
   his joy.

Station Road: Sympathy, Imitation, and Ambition

for Emily Apter

Crossed by three, four, maybe even five creeks in the wet
it will degrade at these low points, and also on the crest
of the rise up past Avonside
                              in its perpetual face-off
with Hathaways;
                  where wandoo dominates
salmon gum, and shade breeds
potholes out of sandy-gravel mix, rutted by tractors
and trucks piled high with hay; a lash of a road
that stretched from Auntie Elsie's
                              at the foot of the Needling Hills
up on Taylor Road, down over the crossroads . . .
it's that simple:
                  in the inculcation of land with Bible — a heavy volume
on the heavy wooden dresser —
                              it simply meant it was the road
that took you from the old homestead,
from the gargoyle augers and compulsive sheep ramps
and their plethoras of *a*-s *aa*-s and *aaa*-s, core of the genealogy,
down to the rail-yard surrounded by bush and paddocks,
rails largely silent.
                  Where Station Road crosses Mackie Road,
we call it The Crossroads . . . Mackie Road and Station Road still
                                        form boundaries
of my cousin Ken's place — a set square to right the rectangle of
                                                  excision:
a greening of the salty lesions.
                              It — The Crossroads — is a place
of strange decision-making, an epistolary interpolation; the locus
to counteract infinite points of stopping, departure, reflection,

distraction, and digression.

Doing three-sixties — doughnuts —
cutting it up — brings on the breakdown quicker here than anywhere:
above it, clouds sprout like mushrooms grown in the grey veins
under the white salt,

and all high places are settled there in a lightning
stroke —

there, we might in situ hear Kalidasa's "The Cloud-
Messenger"
on the tip of our scorched lips . . .

Points of stopping on Station Road
— a soak,
a clump of "finch" trees, a steep-walled dam, the collapsed barn, the
old well . . .
don't add up to an experience of travel.

Neither are they visitation.
Down near Uncle Jack's old place — Avonside —

there's an amazing
bottle pit

— blue bottles, marble-stoppered bottles, torpedoes,

embossings

of vine leaf clusters, bunches of grapes.

The pleasures of digging
are offset by disturbance as well — random shootings,
chemical spillage, breakaways appearing
where the land is barely elevated
enough to support a chasm: inlaid,

they break along perforation lines
held together by anecdotes blithely — if affectionately —
renaming the totems.

To reiterate: this road is not a road was not a
road
to children, but a place of hesitations and digressions. To walk its
edges
before the widening was to shadow utility,

                                   to paraphrase work
and make play; the sheep straggling outside the wires,
faces warm and addictive, lips soft
as anything you shouldn't touch,
                           so readily sucking a finger: eyes so
out there just seeing must risk damage, up against the wire
to get back in, to pin the strands apart
with a forked stick, a down-stroke of wandoo,
                                a greyed bone
to hold apart the points of fusion
in the separated dream; to stand back, outflank, and slowly
suggest them through,
                    a nudging and a rush like feeding,
though they might be in their last season of shearing.
                             And termite mounds
and hollowed trees with nests
                  active year after year:
nest-robbers,
            decapitated grass-trees,
                  the sinking down to The
                         Crossroads
where the salt grew; where my uncle would turn right and drive
down to Mount Hardy Station to collect my mum
visiting her sister during school break,
                      across the Quairading Road,
into the rail-yard . . . once she overshot, asleep
with the infiltrating harvest air,
                  on down to Green Hills where
my uncle was waiting,
             having realised her error, her lapse, her shock
                        on waking,
playing his farmer's hunch, utility reinforced
on the drive down Station Road.

Sympathy – Bogged

1 FRONT VIEW

Heavy vehicle broad grin, tilted.
          Bogged — no traction.
Back wheels down to the axles.
          Bogged — no traction.
The artistry of submersion,
Barely detectable from front-
          On, dark clouds rolling overhead.
          Bogged — no traction.

2 SIDE VIEW

Sympathise – he's down on his knees.
          Bogged — no traction.
Spirit level bubble ascends.
          Bogged — no traction.
Low-geared he tries to ease it out,
Semi-grip then centrifugal
          Rip, spinning wildly, flywheel blitz.
          Bogged — no traction.

3 REAR VIEW

Deluge of Judgement — lateral.
          Bogged — no traction.
Incrementally dropping — cored.
          Bogged — no traction.
Illusion, merging verticals
And horizontals, tail-light sludge
          And embers — collapsed stars — buried.
          Bogged — no traction.

Black-shouldered kite hovers — faint light.
              Bogged — no traction.
Frayed tow-rope stretched between red cars.
              Bogged — no traction.
Ghost figures direct the action.
The triangle shifts, breaks angle.
        Old rope conducts — red on red, mud.
           Towed out — traction.

Of the Effects of Tragedy

Read and forget and try to remember,
like thinking the car will make it through the endless
puddle to get to the edge of Yenyenning Lake
and the front-wheel drive taking it up to the axles,
stranded out where winter brings few,
burgeoned with saline water . . . feeding the Avon;
a close call, that one — seriously close,
my heart in my mouth but not letting the kids
feel the stress — a picnic blanket from the boot
lined the wallowing trench of the left steerer,
then easing the weight of the car onto this cradle,
then shifting into reverse and hitting
the accelerator, a dog-leg jerk-back that shoots you
around 180 degrees — almost — and back on the straight
and narrow, just pause enough to notice the antediluvian
lushness of dead swamp trees in their hundreds,
even thousands, all those greywood surgical
instruments sticking up, a horror through unfiltered
light to bring your children into as the only tract
of "nature" about — farmland sinkhole
laced with sheep skeletons worn down to interiors
by heavy-duty salinity; these clashing
images act as warning — an active-dynamic
kind of warning offset and yet complemented
by the tawny frogmouths' disconcerting whistle
a few hours before dawn, a straining
and drawing through of darkness,
a widely parted divider marking circlets
on tinplate, or a shedding York gum
limb, as hard as beak cartilage; I delayed the typing
of this poem by a few days, not able to formulate
my exact meaning, or thrive on my errors

and then I was going to utilise Burke's image of a fallen
London as one more enticing to those who might never
visit in its "glory", and not actually wishing
collapse, would find annihilation, the remnant of its
immensity, a thrill, frisson, delight . . . a prompt to consider
their own mortality—a lens for the night-song
of the tawny frogmouth? And then, London *was* bombed.
We sympathise with those who suffer having suffered ourselves.
We "delight"? *We* watch vicarious. *We* count the miles
between road houses. The variables twist through personal
disasters like gravel roads. We feel for others
as others would feel for us? Four friends I know of
were near the explosions—at King's Cross Station,
near Russell Square where I lived for three or four months
once . . . I am trying to identify that bird song—I know
it's of a small species . . . just outside the window,
though I can't catch a glimpse of it in the foliage.
Reconfiguring the news on radio, and later
"literature" that mimics and keens our reflections
on "where we were when" . . . Kennedy was assassinated,
or Pink Floyd reformed for the G8 bonanza
on African poverty—an African venue
added at the last moment, an afterthought . . .
Yenyenning partially seen after enduring rains
is ghostly turned inside out, a mass of defeated
photons glittering about the dead . . . kind of withdrawn,
sucked down below the grey glass surface . . . the actors—
snakes here—in an edgy hibernation as winters
are increasingly warmer and the plentiful rain
an aberration.
       They talk about seepage from cemeteries,
but when the dead have been scattered and denied rights,
they drain slowly from the surface, welling in an arterial
layer not far below the growing soil, and move even uphill
down towards sinkholes like Yenyenning—artesian, they

are tapped and rejected, they are trained down to the sea
and ridden mid-winter by powerboats and canoes,
white-watered through rapids, cascades
down through the Avon to the Swan River,
reclaimed down towards the city, gradually
emptied into the sea where concentration is enough now
to be detected if tested in the appropriate way;

                                     what fails
as seepage almost rises up to aerial absolution, though is caught
in the invisible and wiry canopy of sapless trees,
a field of parallel radiation cocooning, thwarting
escape. These actors in their mimicry, despondent.

                                          Stranded,
in universal affection we consider the long walk
over fences and paddocks to the nearest farmhouse: a phone, landline.
It seems more real, less fictive, more powerful.
The bite of isolation — no "flight plan" of where
we might have gone, have ended up — where they'd
have to go to find us if the alarm were raised . . .
fifty ks downriver, off *their* section of the map.

                                          Heavily
armed, young men out here *will* torture — the threat
of violence comes downwind — they walk towards you
and you hear nothing, across bare fields,
down gravel roads, across salty water.

                                     My sympathy
comes out of having been hunted down on more than one
occasion as a young man — my brother and others
are witnesses to this. My brother and I have been hunted
together. This is the dictatorship of the rural
not countenanced in rural safety advertisements
for children: drowned, killed by machinery, motorbikes,
guns . . . riding in the backs of utilities,
tossed out on rough ground, or skylarking
and letting go.

All are participants in this gusting wind . . .
York gum canopies bending and whiplashing
to points of snapping, even the thin dead trees
moving their short duress to breaking point,
their foliage the dead partially rising, and in part,
as mentioned in an earlier hodographic act.
The snakes, restless,
                    whisper in their stillness
what I've always heard as Deo favente,
                              but then,
on the run, I've often ascribed, often
given thanks for deodends
living and dead.
                 When nation as past tense
presumes a tone pattern, prayers to its abstraction
will act as beacons to Yenyenning, cast as language group
across the broader state, the country, with even
cars bogged to the axles, or single men
in lone farm-houses kinned by trauma
elsewhere, washing the roots and tearing the foliage
of trees planted to hold it back,
        to prevent the sapless
delighting in those
              with less.

Imitation Spatialogue

"I shall not defend Rowleys Pastoral: its merit can stand its own defence — "

    T. Chatterton, To Horace Walpole, 14 April 1769 (First draft)

Some months have passed since the Yenyenning track
proved impassable and I was lucky to get the car
and the kids out of the salty sludge;
                         returning,
the ski-boat fraternity has turned out in force,
       and one of the original reasons
for the damnation of the Avon —
                    the saline
choke-out of Yenyenning —
              is reiterated.
      Tailgating us in their four-wheel drives,
their inland dry speedboat travesties home in
on the main lake.
           Aim: to rip it up, drink beer.
            Depth is not great
but enough to ski
      and certainly resplendent to waterbirds
           even if the bush in the surrounding reserve
is a villainy of the dead
      where polemics accumulate
           and some enjoy global warming;
                      looping
straight back out of there,
      also to get the kids out (less so the car), we —
us this time —
      want to avoid

confrontation with the vandals
when they've set their scene,
created their combat zone;
the issue
of the lake —
vestigially inherent
but forced into shape
by damming and manipulation,
is one of intrinsic curvature —
otherwise known as Gaussian curvature:
ostensibly,
I feel the strength of *their* —
the skiers and drinkers
and bush bashers —
harnessing the waters of the lake
lies in their confidence
that it is curved in the shape of a bowl,
that the product K
(intrinsic curvature)
is positive
because k_1 and k_2
share a negative sign;
I sense they are wrong,
and that a heavy winter
means the bowl has buckled,
that the floor of the lake has saddled
along the lines of k_1+, k_2-; $K-$,
or, even more extremely
with a monstrousness
actively preparing
to rise up
on the balmy late spring day —
a subscription of agency
to the much maligned and abused lake itself —
$+N$ upwards, k_1-, k_2+; $K-$;

of course,
                    I have the visual representation
in my mind's eye,
            or, if needs be,
            in Graham Nerlich's *The Shape of Space*,
            to fall back on:
                            if the ski-boys only knew
            how much
they could get out of considering
the unlimited two-space of the body —
                                    Nerlich noting:
                    "if we overlook the holes, for the sake of simplicity
and, perhaps, decency) . . ."
                            which leaves you and me and the kids —
us — hightailing it out of there,
            out past the deadly blue of the lake/s,
the crown-of-thorns-work of dead trees —
                                    a species lasting longer
dead than alive,
            the warped track and 1-form
                    up and down imaging
as the wheels shock-undulate
            across the contours and rides
of the cattle grids;
                    and noticing the Gaussian issue
applying to the sky
            which is saddling downwards,
                    or maybe breaking out
of this into other spatialities:
                            bending into topological meltdown;
holding our hands out against the windscreen,
            a windscreen cracked by stones
                    kicked up by tracks and trailers,
star fields not yet linked
                    by superstition;

we awaited —
                await and will await —
                                the extrusion
or fold
        that'll absorb our impact:
                we wonder if it's affecting the skiers,
if it's knocked them off their precarious and rapid perches,
                                                if they'll
even notice it was more than a drop in speed,
                        a loss of balance,
        too much to drink;
                                warding-off, a branch on the road
brings us to ground —
                        we stop, I lift and toss it
to the side of the road,
        collect the fragments,
                drive on
distracted from the sky
        by an old concrete silo on a bare hill,
its vacant bounty,
                and to take it in
        we bend on our seats
as if they were knees
        to look up at an increasing
and past angle —
                in this case,
        though thinking of the Klein bottle,
                                        our *in actual fact*
unmoving knees predicated to the left, and up, and closing, and lost,
are not homomorphic;
                        the skiers bend their knees
                in control, or loss,
        edging up,
                especially at take-off,
                        the blue salt waters

                                    washing over the ridge,
into the river system;
                                we notice ring-necked parrots
                curving down, grounded, corellas
unable to rise
                more than the height
        of the silo, trees;
                                we surmise
fresh and saltwater aquatic animals
        rising near to the surface —

                                        the instabilities
of sky's curvature
        keeping us all close
at hand.

The Last of England

No old-country nerves,
no mothering tongue
Gorgon nation, as steady forward,
homunculus reaching out
of midriff, a gentle grip,
hand clasp to cloy cold copy,
facsimile expectation,
longer than cabbage will supply.

Husband paws
the palette, brimming
El Dorado, to soil the sea, cliff's
epiphany — bleached, passé,
stagnant genealogy. Warped
as sailors, rosy-cheeked —
a Madonna's chilly nature;
and *so* the avant-garde: Napoleonic

shock troops,
Malory's knights
in heavy armour. Blitzkrieg.
Virtue fleeing Egypt — white
horses, gold gathered, the British Museum —
what have we left, to flee census,
creditors, antiphonal lash
of caricature, blast of northern airs.

PART II

Astonishment
(Of the Passion Caused by the Sublime)

A tract of bush without twists and loops
of dumped product, dead sheep, mounds
of beer bottles, settlement weeds clinging
to a hillside, a single cell of bush concentrating
attention; the rumble of a V8 on bitumen
not far from where you explore a sandy
track, your car parked a short way
into clumps of hakea, where a V8 slowing down
is warning — taking an interest in banksias
unlikely – the driver glimpsing, processing
brakes and deceleration, those crimes
opportunity and the grotesque feed on,
circumstantial paths almost joined.

Closer to home, bring unreachable wandoos
on the steepest side of Walwalinj closer . . .
binoculars welded to glasses, to eyes . . .
more intense than being there, taste of terror
enlarged unfamiliar but still perspective
a subject held in the palm of a trickster,
lens his medium, not mechanism,
branching vein structure, brain tissue,
flume of lymph, vertical fan coral
prised out of sediments, the familiar
you barely notice though birds fly up in flocks
and disappear, all colours absorbed — pink and grey,
green-blue-yellow-orange plash of twenty-eights,
minute red-capped robins carrying red
further than background edicts.

In this perverse travelling, lived-in countries
form overlapping triptychs despite oceans . . .

topographies of differing personality traits,
a single image welded and transmogrified,
pungent bacilli you can barely rest up in,
that troubles with comfort of sparrow
or ant trails, blue-tongue lizard lodged
tight in winter sleep: it reminds you,
the smallest difference on re-encounter
astonishes, fills you with that terror,
a salivation of ensconcement,
heteromorph's vision of exile,
roots tapped deeper than rock,
teasing flick or rustled hairline.

Terror

Valency of first driving solo with mates
and racing a railway crossing late at night, orange
light of refineries, paddocks scarcely perceptible,
stereo crackling with distortion, and cutting
it close enough to alter friendships, curtail
the creepy road movie; to inculcate and twist
an axle, impose caesura: masculine fairytales
of sheet-metal and rare orchids, machinery and nature.

Or boating out to Africa Reef and suddenly, heavy seas . . .
sheer, perpendicular, keeping broadside temptation
bow-first, forced to buoyancy or wreckage . . . surviving
vessel is drawn to trailer on making harbour,
friends and friend's father — captain — silent
in temporality, lost in brute angles of water,
its weight, visceral content, face after face crumpled.

The depth of swell vertical and horizontal,
properties of embodiment, chopping muscles:
analysis can unpick the belly — birth swell
of savage fluids, amniotic undoing of bonds
as specific as flesh, even sucked-dry bone:
as now, inland is a slow heaving, and here
we feel slight earthquakes often, knowing

in our earthquake-flexible-dwelling,
that a BIG ONE is sure to come, this language
of disaster seaming agitation, "putting food
on the table", blurring cultural comparatives
like aperitifs of intactness, laying out utensils —
an anthropological racket — selling point
at prime time when the dusty rubble of houses
hit by hellfire rockets are hillocks in a desert.

Clearness

Small-town bank fate awaits those breaking even,
Not increasing overall value-adding;
Junior councillor profits nicely, old man
        Divvies property.

Looking out from here on a clear day, desert
Frays the edge of the picture . . . crops and scrub blur,
Die out . . . fluid fails while ag-business, parrots,
        Scarcely grow. Mining.

Sky-flex falsifies perception, so fixed on
Windscreens, windows, telescopic sights, portals,
Divination, they take the straight and narrow
        Out of . . . here; fixate.

Like Power

Tandem air-seeder cling-gripping
duality of wheel-sink,
                        no Satan *here*
                        is majestic in his pomp,
all the gear possessed by masters and their
apprentices, all flames-thrown
called "burning-off";

                        Beverley kids hate Yorkies,
though a topiaried Y vanished or vanquished
from slow-down drive in hark, hale, or greeting,
will render
                inland town of ORK replete
                with Orkies,
displaced in heritage alignments —
Okies have satellite and Orkney visits
make hard copy;
                evidence is local news;

Autumn flowers bloom on trellises
                entering town;
the river gluts and car-buffs
                        pilgrimage like salt
hidden beneath the wash;

Poisoners draw up contracts
                                for down-track
wardings-off,
        mis-spent bridges
                        ease on gantries — pylons
        the soldiers
of parataxis, like voting

held at the school; it's why bikies
without patches induce no terror
outside Café Bugatti;
                                  rigid initiations
untaming auto responses
to sex and what suits
            the local pleasures;

those threatening foxes, dragging
chunks of the dead around
                                  like what
Jakobson said
about Xlebnikov's syntax.

Privation

Deprived, as in waste or wastage
                              seed scatterings
where shattered stalks dropped and winnowed, a district
windrowed;
                 and so allayed, in semi-solitude, semi-silence,
shades filtering through darkened turnings,
                                            a sway
having need of,
             as roused in sedition
                 a mandatory seven years' imprisonment,
or even up to:
             shoot to kill,
             this merging of creed and derivation,
of *equipmental* wastage,
                          slumbering of equipment
reliably truthful:
                 and so,
             as blankly useful; and so, needs must . . .
in strife, they sign away designate assign signify
             and signature white gums like ballot boxes
                 on the Lakes-to-York run, these forest-fearing
vandals whose spray-can equipment is shoddy
             in its artworked affinity, defence 'capabilities';
                                            where loss of scene
or vista
             might eventually stir up compassion:
                                            our loss
is their loss is your loss is our loss is compunction;
                                            John
                 builds a new bed-head
for the metal bed so Timmy won't get limbs stuck
exploring,

a liberation as deprived of space
in the cot he's outgrown,
                    he walks warily — side by side with us —
cautious of snakes; as edited — a privation akin to *Vacuity, Darkness,
Solitude*
and *Silence* . . .
                    Spring is slow getting started
at the 'gateway' . . . it's usually over
                              before it begins — a brief prelude
to brutally hot summers;
                              late rains
have meant high grass —
                    snakes
are appearing in record numbers . . .
                    yesterday, a gwarder
up the driveway, this morning
          a juvenile dugite
                    on the veranda . . .
                                        a few days back,
                              a four-foot dugite
          crossed a few inches in front of Timmy . . .
                                             mesmerized
by the liquid flick
          of the snake's seamless body; as travelling
          for your betterment — self-improvement —
                    you get it in planes, that massive loss, terrible
self-doubt, doubting the equipment, company, world . . . decay,
withdrawal;
               here, day birds sing at night
               as out of kilter as the seasons,
and farmers
          who don't think they're responsible
                              for turning the rivers
saline — or as their parliamentary representatives
                              claim:

et inania *regna*,
this solemn empire that stretches wide around,
Mr Pitt on the floor, the Missile Crisis still
unresolved in Cuba.

Vastness: A Glimpse of Alaska

I AN IDEA OF ALASKA

I'm told you shouldn't see McKinley
from here, despite its size. It's an optical
trick, a lens effect and clear skies
out to the right. This land-grab is full of space,
and snow this late fills between trees
like sand drifts — here, ambition
is braced by mountains.

Roads are scarce, and *that* we can celebrate.
They haven't branched and spread
as roads will do, and the highway
is a single artery-vein through which blood
flows and backwashes with the same beat.
Small planes fly low to Inuit settlements
dealing with their own stories.

All eyes look North, the Arctic Circle
a centrifuge. A truckie I know says the highway
will eat a set of tyres, and that Barrow's
toughest oil men are eaten alive
by its endless night. American, but separate,
they come from everywhere,
and talk about Ohio like it's home.

Yes, I can see McKinley,
its hypnotic off-centring. In summer
mosquitoes swarm about the cabins
just out of town, and I think
of the old tales I won't be told.

The oil pipeline not as large
as one might think.

Soon, random claims
for settling will reach into the heart
of the Interior, where a hunter and his mate
saw a Bigfoot, hirsute and hunched,
study them before running — an Alaskan
with its own names for place, its own claims
of "unexplored territory".

2 THE DREDGE

Spat out polished stones:
hardly lashed to the banks,
just bogged down;
still ice-bound the river ran its course
through the belly of the dredge: all-in extractor
of the river's golden teeth, this iron behemoth
so over the top, evolutionary end
of the industrial urge;
no description can render its majestic
metal tackiness, its gigantism
into more than the mounds of stones
we perch on, sinews of cable
and awkward beak and orifices
supreme in their effectiveness:
a river turned inside out.
Having said this, suspect
its ghost is small;
it rings hollow
when a stone
is thrown, and Dutch courage
turns to an assault against all things metal;
the tenacity of seedlings

and nourishment of moose droppings
will outplay four-wheelers
ripping along the paths,
drinking hard down by the road,
and stone-fall is the will
of the river calling back
its own — the sun out,
the wind brisk, just cold.

3 ANCHORAGE AIRPORT

Mountains brace the runway
like Kathmandu. The great
white hunter lives here:
world record Kodiak Brown Bear —
taxidermy by . . . bold
as its skull width.

Opposing case:
the last year polar bears
were taken, the good Dr
bagged this whopper, world
record, skull width, *taxidermy by* . . .
up on hind legs, poised
to come down through the plastic,
to come down on the hunter's
wife, children, patients — out there,
where records were made,
so human those bears,
so sentinel, so poised
traveller's comment,
waiting for their flights,
the mountains at their backs
less vast than they are.

Journal (Vastness)

On Albert Tucker's "Explorers Fording River"

So gnarl, press on,
  not weaken befores or afters,
 make haven in waste, gazette
   extinctual scan as chips
off older blocks – riverviews
 unbecome a surge of ghosts in trunks,
blotch of scruples in canopy, sky

  as blue as eyes
   streaked white once were –
 glowing finance of our backers,
   corrugated Knights Templar,
 mountless roughriders, press on
in khaki flow, jut-jaw belligerance,
as declared – scientific – garrulous

  it is said of us,
   heroicise our brutals?
 Alone, trudging solipsists, grace
   and glide arterials, ford the aura
 silted bed, mirror narratives flat, press on,
 reflectionless, prised of shadow, waver
in flesh: let them come on, and on,

  shoulder arms, fall
   divided where wagons
 fail to circle – no fear! unslung
   metal backbone, shudder
 riparian swathes of pollen,
 our drive to mine a visage: seams
of fauna riven deep to characters. Press on.

Lover's Leap

"There was a promontory in Acarnania called Leucate, on the top of which was a little temple dedicated to Apollo. In this temple it was usual for despairing lovers to make their vows in secret, and afterwards to fling themselves from the top of the precipice into the sea, where they were sometimes taken up alive. This place was therefore called the Lover's Leap; and whether or no the fright they had been in, or the resolution that could push them to so dreadful a remedy, or the bruises which they often received in their fall, banished all the tender sentiments of love, and gave their spirits another turn; those who had taken this leap were observed never to relapse into that passion. Sappho tried the cure, but perished in the experiment."

"C", from *Spectator*, No. 223, Thursday, November 15, 1711

Lifting off from the cliffs of Leukas, once again
am I tumbling into the gray sea, drunk with desire.

Anacreon (2nd half of the 6th C.), Fragment 376 (trans. John Porter)

Effusions. As over the softer edge
the harsh waters burned. A green effusion,
to dash as rocks — hyphens
in bleak spread of remembrances,
lines of fences so under our view cross
the rolling hills: appear, reappear, occluded.
As if once in your life a word repeated — a moniker, a catch-all —
finds its perfect moment: pure
application. Hand held lone to the clouds, the river swerving
behind you, the vestige of a road; from down there
a granite roughneck, a collar of jags
that while interesting
is nothing dramatic . . . The impact is away,

and cloistered, or like an amphitheatre, a drama in which the audience
is argued male, and yet here we are, two sides of the self,
the liminal equivocation that queers horizons,
that makes rounded the panorama.

We should have taken that painting down,
awkward in the living room; hanging crooked. "Near
Heidelberg" by Arthur Streeton — a shoddy reproduction,
some other history from a distant place
that reminds us vaguely of here,
what it was like when the family
looked over the paddocks, before the rabbits came in numbers.
I agree: it's not of here. I agree. It's someone else's history,
or maybe no one's history at all.
Just another painting that hides the truth,
makes affable the decline of shade. Here, it's like moorland
from our holiday in Yorkshire — a few stunted trees,
sheep points of a shape frustrating geometry. But only just an allegory,
chips of paint lost to roughness and haphazard texture
when viewed too close. You preferred Borobudur,
the shadow puppets of Java.

"INFINITY, though of another kind, causes much of our pleasure
in agreeable, as well as of our delight in sublime, images. The spring
is the pleasantest of the seasons; and the young of most animals,
though far from being completely fashioned, afford a more agree-
able sensation than the full-grown; because the imagination is enter-
tained with the promise of something more, and does not acquiesce
in the present object of the sense. In unfinished sketches of drawing,
I have often seen something which pleased me beyond the best finish-
ing; and this I believe proceeds from the cause I have just now
assigned."

Edmund Burke, "Infinity in pleasing Objects".

45

We're laced together by the dry and waterways, the patterns
of watershed and capillary; in the few books we've ordered for the
shelves
we hoped to fill, it repeats as adage "we were meant to be",
or destined, or doomed, or just fatalities cauterised in the ebb and
flow
of parenthetical tributaries; polished like a skull
that moss has settled on, it's a familiar
view of the infinite: the spring lambs
shivering on their wonky pinions,
nuzzling mothers still worn down by birth,
inducted into the summer's mirage-driven heat; the infinite
only gives you a space persistently looking back, the completed
sketch
the scene before we began observing; the sun drawn close
to your skin, you burn severely, and winter becomes the season
of redemption, and we will bear winter children.

In reclaiming — taking the moment in hand,
we hold the full weight of our hearts; a grasp they might
not prise apart, so welded, as tactile as focus,
the single, unique gnat in a swarm,
convulsive clouds configuring the horizon; what
would we say wound back? What manners
displayed after culture has left us: this clash of vapours,
frustration at the ghostly self being just membranous
enough to notice, get caught in the cleft of granite
yawning at the base of the leap. It's so local,
the lethargy keeping us here until gravity
fragments, shifts. Where will it take us? To accept
the spirits of those we recognise are stuck in their places
of death: those here won't acknowledge us,
or don't hear us, or listening out for their living kin
remain distracted, entirely focused.

If only those moving through — the corporeal — knew
how loud, how deafening their prayers
can be, they'd say them less often? Maybe, maybe not.
After all, they listen for their echo.

A Difficult First Harvest. Wheat Variety: Carnamah

for Ken

I COSMOLOGY: FROM A REPORT ON THE SOUTHERN SKIES

I see the Saucepan — Orion's belt —
as you crunch stubbled clods after breaking up
and think the gradient of land
and flow of water and salt feathering
from the place where creeks start.
I drift as if come down from the cab
of the tractor unable to grip boot on rippled iron step,
and slipping don't hit the mirror-shatter of the ground
taking light in and reflecting the Handle as Orion's sword,
the ploughshares as weapon conflation that's like conscription,
the handle's rivet the Orion nebula, *which is visible*
to the naked eye under clear skies.
Above bright — Rigel, below Betelgeuse.
I see Andromeda, I imagine alpha (triple star) and beta Centauri,
I see no nations in the Southern Cross, in religious empires
alpha and gamma Crucis, beta and delta Crucis, horizontal line
that stays on the screen as we watch the news,
despite the upgrading of transmissions in the country,
the antennae on Mount Bakewell boosting
only partially through the dust and flecks of dead and burnt wheat
stalks
from last year's crop, when this block was leased
out to another family under the full-spread
of southern skies, last light of star maps eaten by disk plough
crossing of the cross /coal sack/ bright cluster also.

2 EARTH

Red loams legumed prior and spatial soil-mapped
holding water too much in parts but reasonable
drainage dissected laterite
wandoo nudged out of thick soil
clay-based catchment for residual chemicals
nitrogenous headiness, urea in the folds
of hand picked clods held up and whiffed for decomposition
of organic matter with even here higher up a touch of salt
but not enough to thwart a hardy variety of wheat
like Carnamah not so thirsty though rain in the valley
comparatively good: in the grand scheme of things.

3 GETTING THE CROP IN . . .

Think there'll be follow-up rains . . .
Don't want to leave it too late, nor go too early . . .
Don't want to have to reseed and get a stunted delivery . . .
Think there'll be follow-up rains . . .
And the ground isn't too boggy . . .
Have cleaned the seeder and got in the fertiliser . . .
Using a mixture of chemical and this "natural" stuff . . .
A kind of plant mulch as alternative . . .
Giving it a go, but not all the way . . .
Think there'll be follow-up rains . . .
Wouldn't mind one of those fancy air-seeders one of these days . . .
Not enough acres to justify the outlay . . .
Though maybe one day . . .
Think there'll be follow-up rains . . .

4 AND KEEPING IT GOING . . .

Fungus this year . . .
they're aerial spraying

though we're trying
to use less spray
or maybe no spray
but the government
insists it's nipped
in the bud.
Wouldn't it slay ya!
Rains have been patchy
but adequate,
frosts light.
As Alphonse Karr said,
"Plus ça change,
plus c'est
la meme chose" . . .
I don't know
if he knew
anything
about pesticides,
herbicides,
and fungicides.

5 FOUR COLOUR THEOREM OF DRYING CROPS

Only four colour tones of drying crops are needed
to differentiate them in such a way that no two adjacent crops
share the same colour tone four times against the border
and no single point being relevant as deflected across
that point the stramineous or florescent will maintain
or interchange upsetting the ears pale green or yellowing
or bisque or even lime if shades of colour
against the prism of wheatstalks glinting reflective
in drying quadrilateral three times being inadequate
and five times seemingly provable as too many
in the red rust shine of crop failure or the colourless
absorbency of ears that don't ripen don't plump

under the bite of the spring sun and wilt
into neighbouring crops so nothing's adjacent
just blurred in the four sectors of hue.

6 THE TAINTS OF HARVEST

If rats run riot through the header and auger
the night before harvest then there's no telling
in the loud silence of wheat rippling
on a clear late spring day, the blue
canopy a comb that'll run through eight bags an acre
of choice Carnamah with good protein,
the crunch of stubble behind the cut
as the tractor ruts in the off-cuts,
no telling that a single dropping
hidden below the dunes of rich gold-ochre
in the loaded truck will bring
the wrath of wheat board and neighbours
like all plagues rolled into one,
that reprieve is the seed-cleaners
at Quairading and the willingness
to fix the one-load error,
to cop it on the chin
and get back out there,
bringing crystal-clean wheat
to the bin, the coffers of the district.

7 POST-

I see the Saucepan — Orion's belt —
as you crunch stubbled clods after breaking up
and think the gradient of land
and flow of water and salt feathering
from low ground, place where creeks start . . .

Wave Motion Light Fixed and Finished

Light carves a surface;
Light anneals fibres;
Light reflects and polishes;
Light collects in red gums;
Light infuses the river-mouth;
Light surfs rock and sand;
Light caught outside focuses in the studio;
Light's harmonics; Light's deletions;
Light's semi-tones of shadow;
silver parcels of sky-light; panels like prayer mats;
silver-leaf leaves flattened rolled out luminous ignition of solar
panels cloud formational reprise and a top-dressing finished glance;
ergo sum, ergo sunt, ergonomics of steel-pinned beauty,
Freida Kahlo strength, the saw bench, saw-light, wound
healing as wood planed to river loop and stretch, upwind
                                                    downstream
filaments of trees reaching into salt-freshwater rendition, to walk
on black foil lift-off surface tension skip a beat
fish jump in largesse of cloud, tonnage of water vapour
as carved out old laws and coastal raiders
as fourteenths of a whole, holistically challenging to float above
a bed of wood, a bed of air, a bed of light, as solid as erosion from
southerlies cutting into hamlets and guilds,
a code, a tapping of branch on branch we might think
vaguely light Morse code this small part we can see at once
of any vision, any transmutation of heightened emotion, the variable
light of idea, sketch, rough, and finished product, artefact, item,
                                                    example,
distillation . . . an economy of presence, an evidence of passing
                                        through the waves
of horizon, the highs and lows of occupation . . . silver nitrate tint,
                                                    Polaroid

caught out before exposure, lightning-driven trees lit up like
                                        superstition, anatomy
interface grain reaching across planar quelling of spilt tea, spilt coffee,
blackbutt counteraction, storm-fallen revivification, as if each cell in
                                        its harmonic
is charging for renewal, the divan the ocean we slide into, nesting
chairs called back to the same spot to amplitude, sine wave
that lopes scansion bevelled edges tanged to ferrel and groove,
to sit and look out at imprints of rapture or haunting, luminous fire-
                                        wrought
hardened stock and buffer zone, delay contact consumed and melded
to carry out day-to-day activities, concentrate on one aspect of
                                        revelation,
a music emanates as light over ripples and echo-soundings
of wood density and rock density and water density and the sunset
                                        off-cuts
of light dampened, the temple stretched, this slow-time analysis of
                                        decompression,
emerging from within the element, the bends bring contract
and oxygen does something else, here the bends are absorbed, you
                                        flow
with them emergence, the night-eyes not seen as steel glints
a fine line, spirits of night falter on light borders withdrawing or
                                        creeping
into the vista, a front blown out, sleep bandwidth in the silent sound
                                        system,
the pin dropping so loud in distillation; pragmatically, light moves
                                        across the table,
pragmatically, light fills the wall behind the canvas, the floor and
                                        walls
light-heavy, light-drenched; changeable, flighty, instant, light thrills
the horizon, thrills the sharp lines
outside the halo, runs riot, and river flows on
and the furniture in the bedroom, living room, lounge room, dining
                                        room . . .

settles; going out . . . work, a show, a walk . . . a sense of where
                                                        things sit
stays with you, side-step, accommodate, meld . . . as seagull, osprey,
                                                        sooty
oyster-catchers, criss-cross and throw up solar panels, throw up
                                                        diffuse
maps of absolute light; in the land's curvature, the shark swims
                                                        through
the territory of roo and wallaby, heavy-bodied cows light on their
                                                        feet,
up to the river's edge, forests breathing moistly; the lamps shifts and
                                                        haunted
trees emerge, or figures of the dispossessed — they can't be built out,
textured into the immensity of ocean and sky and headland,
low wattage of sunset driven up over rise, silhouette intensifying
where we walked, where all have walked out of memory,
taking sustenance out of the reconfigured picture,
having been there before and before; a line of herring
race the coastline, heavier fish sit close to the bottom, poised
on the edge of our seats, the table floats on silver air, the sky
made horizontal, the horizon a vertical line attaching
ceiling and floor — no vertigo comes with this, or searching out
                                                        vertigo
it is a sonorous warmth of blended specificity: light peaking and
                                                        dropping,
crests and troughs, concurrent and ecliptic,
the certainty of form when solar activity upsets the animals, confuses
bio-rhythms, the certainty of the shape waking to look out over the
                                                        same space,
sunspots ripping through heath and forest, sizing canvas and coating
the hard dead growth, a form of rekindling
the ups and downs of days alone, days full of shadow, days burning
                                                        with glare
and a brooding atmosphere, days becalmed, days where a memory
forced down below the surface, planes of light, bursts out

like caught sun, and then settles back into the dimensions
of the domestic, the pastoral: light transfigures, regenerates, blinds;
light is not to be taken for granted; light's properties grow
in the limestone caverns where we haven't seen, the sea connected
with where we stand, or sit, or spread ourselves out to float or hover
or petrify or sink down into surfaces below surfaces
and perspectives of light, thin membrane of land carved by seven

waves
then seven waves and so on, on one side and lightly so on, on the

other
more circumstantial though never casual the repetitions of wave

motion,
river lappings carried against the banks against the skin-drum, against
Light's semi-tones of shadow;
Light's harmonics; Light's deletions;
Light caught outside focuses in the studio;
Light surfs rock and sand;
Light infuses the river-mouth;
Light collects in red gums;
Light reflects and polishes;
Light anneals fibres;
Light carves a surface . . .

Light: King of the Burnout Shows Full Range of Emotions

Having written his letter in rubber,
tyres popping after five ks of rioting,
he walked the dead quiet road
of his accomplishment, the seven
colours of the evening sky
throwing a spectral
argument out of alignment,
refraction of blue light
scuffing boots
greasy with lanoline,
camouflage of beer stains
shape-shifting over his shirt,
tobacco-stained fingers
grabbing at mosquitoes
orbiting his handiwork,
zigzag polyautography,
stone heart buzzing
with bed-talk, with early-rising
nightjars and peccadilloes,
signing off like bliss
vulcanised "dark
with excessive light"
as what he thinks
it might be.

Colours of the Wheatbelt

If all colours therein are to be found in the spectral tail-feathers
of a 28 parrot, so are they to be found in the flickering slither
of a juvenile dugite, come into the house through an uncovered
drainpipe, working the polish of the stone-tiled floor
hard for traction, and sending shudders through the air
like a photo taken out of focus so that resonances
of the body shape unfold like an incremental halo
about its form — intentionally. In the half-light
of the corridor the translucent then opaque
olive green gives way to an under-shadow
of night-rich blackness, the ochre of its adult
manifestation a slippage between the overlap of scales,
a body stretching beneath the set weight of its skin,
a place to shelter searched out, senses hard pressed
and the thin darkness of narrow places
a rainbow dense with chemical light
of its touch, the streaming colours within.

Loudness

Faux and yet resplendent, crows gather and garner
open ground, clamouring;
                                                  so intense the updraft, the awakening
of the collective miracle, rapturous uprising,
and yet the sky barely moving, clouds
barely parting — if anything, an inversion, or a foveola,
a gasp of light through porthole or glance,
a clash: shields, thunder, intentions
like killings;
                        jailed, witnesses
cluster in tight-aired places
where candles won't burn, these oubliettes we visit
on television, we turn up to catch
whispers;
                        animal cries or animal noise segues here
like variable Elizabethan spellings, like the Arcadia
manuscript scribed and variant in St John's, or guttered
and arriving, the choked groan of white-faced herons
roosting in flooded gums, herald birds
louder than a contrary breeze, the cold front
just making presence;
                                        gunshot is not the echo that scales
vertebrae like a fox scream or traumatised dog,
running its kennel,
                                or tawny frogmouth croak intensifying
darkness, flashlight capturing extension
of branch or fencepost, the weighted crack
of humidity dragging a limb to the ground faster
than gravity, which is termed approximation
and not the precision taught to us — to me — at school . . .
its lies keep us grounded,
                                        its contrariness encourages

our spirituality . . . loudness relies on the meditative,
the contra-tinnitus of solitude;
                              from this vade-mecum,
a new set of observations, data from experiments
conducted in a vacuum, where coming apart
the heaviest bonded molecules are replete
with silence, are the propulsion of gas
across vocal cords
                    of traumatised cats made feral
by land-clearers and shooting clubs, "Better than 1080"
winning for poetic sveltiness, their quota of dead cats
coming in under crops where "sinister flatness lay";
my place —
            language hovel —
                        harbours
centrifuge and ballistics, and ears damaged since
youth crackle and flutter with the movement of vehicles,
prongs of scarifier; sometimes, I don't know where
to place myself, though darkened rooms
make gentler the loudness of wings, air traffic;
                                          I counter
affection, as between reception
                            touch and luck
are qualities of sound, a death of gravity on the trampoline
drum . . . supersensitised, I could still be brutal
without knowing it, awareness
of clamouring multitudes
brief and massive, forewarning
avalanche where ground is low, and alpine
respectively four hundred and seventy-so metres
of granite weathering,
                        a coming-down of karma,
or spirits of blank sleepings — dreamless and weighed down
by tearing, falling, clashing, colliding,
ricochet, and the steady tapping

of religion, flagrant
                          in late seasonal shift,
                as loud as scales
in the early throes of sleep.

Swoop (suddenness)

Suddenness a parabola, cut of pendulum,
regionalism we'd imagine;
                              a steady line
from road to treeline, deletions
of light breeze, dictions of cloud,
irritations coloured out — idols
of *vicious demonstrations* . . . sweetly
landed; give me a break.
              You take a portion, a magpie's
ripping hardware, parental fire, and curse
the regular: a strengthened dream, prolific
tempering of tabernacle . . .
              And then it's done.
         Leant against skin
of shed, the metal bar toppled, crashed
against raintank, resounded singularly
across the paddock . . .
                         pink and greys
dismounted dead limb, shape-wise still a York gum,
and resettled — to the naked eye, flashing
in knee-jerk reaction, precisely back
to where they started.
                  An alteration,
then continuance, though swooping magpie,
its nesting ire sanctioned, rips again,
intensified, if anything.
              How do you say: prick of a thing,
I admire you . . .?
                  Why bother cosying up to the neighbour
swooping in on his "special materials" wings,
self-deluded "angel of evening".
                  It upsets highly-strung

members of household—a blue enfolding,
white flagged against barbed wire,
                                    raider
moves of magnitude. That's worship
in granary logic—implanting
pleasure, shredding Miltonic absolutes
settled here as warning
                        against a love
                of nature. Apprehend
sundew and scarlet runner, outré
on firebreaks . . .
                    apprehend
this swoop against incursion,
raid of logic: as over *strongholds and defences*,
we parry, shout suddener
        than we rebuild our pictures,
                decorate the senses.

Intermitting

Outside, intermitting thunder;
habituating
                    the place of lightning
a spectrum flourished
                    where wire stretched
                              thirty-three years ago,
just broken through — rust;
              a pair of massive wedge-tailed eagles
flew towards each other then counter-circled,
              creating a cylindrical reservoir,
a dead zone.
                    The unsolved beacon, an avatar,
prodigious interlude,
                              oxidation: here,
                              twenty-three years ago
you walked in pitch black, sensing salmon gum
boundaries, gravel gutters,
              tinge of cold heat
                    buried in fenceline;
distantly, the crossroads, and a single intermittent
light flashing —
                         less than flashing, blinking
dully — a compulsion
                              driving
the heart rate
              up, a languid attraction, low
and tremulous. If you survive, you will travel
far from here.
                    The precision of emittance:
dead centred;
              by squinting, you track
why it is

that cast out, the lexicon
of the Gospel of Mark
comes out
       talismanically:
farm (9–35) . . . unclean (11–31) . . . sinner (6–47) . . .
       gain sight (6–25) . . .?
                  And why it is
       those who worship
don't take the hint:
       tractors bogged down, trying to seed
                  when rain has bucketed down,
unable to come to grips
                        with moisture.
The light, intermitting, is kind of . . . unclean.
You can shift blame
       just like that;
                  just like Harry S. Truman: "The force
from which the sun
       draws its power
                  has been loosed
against those who brought war . . .", just like Einstein.
Light, intermitting, collates violence;
each step closer
       it doesn't strengthen: salivate,
perspire . . .
                  deaths in the Australian bush
take a long time to clear up . . . if ever:
       tin can on gate post
clicks with the easterly, times perfectly,
                  phase-switching . . .
                        four-veined,
vacuumed, a hand held out blackens
and silvers, turns . . . rabbit shooter,
sniper, thrill killer.

Stench

Bogged down in ground now fetid
with continuous rain, prostates playing up
through lack of sunlight,
                                  frustration
of waterlogging, familiarity-bred snakes
                wavering furrows
                         and plough rituals
of galah-hysteria . . . and a stench
                washed up from the deepest dirt, rising up
                         through the wet-black
of solitary tree branches, a stink
that only stops with High Heaven burn-out;
                                              cut dead
                out of hibernation (ploughed, re-ploughed . . .
flooded out of cavities)
                         snakes were summoned
to straighten the bankrupted scrawl,
                summoning the clergy, doctors,
                         but not councillors
who'd fallen from favour,
                                  disgraced
over the abandonment of hypnosis,
bridging
        of salt and fresh water;
                living here now,
active as street arguments or damnations
in chambers, malodorous past.
Are you now,
        have you ever been
out on the shallowing river?
                         Stench builds;
                in the double conscience

Malodour is the name for this place
                people retire to
or take weekenders,
                selling after a few years
        their token sheep wizened, flyblown,
though gardens remarkably tidy.
Malodour
        is what the poor
                along the railway line
term it, accused of vandalism: small town,
news travels fast.
                Are you now, or have you ever been . . .?
Stenc builds —
                an Old English resonance
of more rain
        than run-off can handle:
                "9 years here
        and I wouldn't dare call myself
a local . . ."

                or

                "with no title deeds
to more than seven hundred acres
        I wouldn't dare call myself a farmer . . ."
and so on till the stench of sheep
        dumped in the nature reserve (shit!
what's on the nose? it'd strip paint from the ceiling . . .)
                evolves a community
project: are you now, or have you ever been
a member?

PART III

Proportion not the Cause of Beauty in Plants

Clasping sepals —
Shock valued, lean
Fringed mantis — green
Spider orchids

Outreach and stretch
Columnar, bid
Insects that grid
Pollen, petal

Platform, to land
In woodland, stall
Enfolded, thrall
Of cross-gender.

Niche bushland holds
Generators,
High-wired spurs;
Contraceptive?

As sharp to prick
You, spikes that thrive
On thin stalk, strive:
Counterbalance.

Proportion in Family Portrait in Regional Gallery

Father shorter by a head than his youngest,
Brown dog looming over son, daughter, mother;
Mythology is not Greek, giant sunflowers
      Not native. Small smiles.

Shading tricks the eye into thinking blood-link,
Paterfamilias . . . consanguinity?
Church in background? Sans crucifix and stained glass?
      Minuscule. Bright, though.

Sister, brother, entwined about each other —
Feet to torso, thin hands barely able to
Ward off father's gnashing teeth. Massive sun shape
      No light source. Windmills.

Gradual Variation

The bird rings the changes; introducing a line,
a steady progression from head to neck to wings to tail,
with some angling in flight, a gradual variation: a black-shouldered
                                                              kite,
or a twenty-eight parrot in its swinging voyage, slammed by a family
                                                              sedan,
ricocheting . . . all angles . . . transitions ruffled, upending the
                                                        glistening
gum leaves which Old Man Wheeler always said portended rain;
the kids got car-sick even a few miles out of sight of the mountain . . .
the speculation of landmarks, historic buildings like the Castle Pub
to be fast-food chained, so weekend visitors can connect
the shortening road between city and country . . . can enjoy
this new focal point of aviator aviatrix avi-top-dressing
                                                    invigilation . . .
land-owners, in smoothing over the hills — denuded of trees, granite
                                                        exfoliations
decapitated, outcrops picked bare, smooth as the even flow of air
over a consistent material over thousands of years — simulated beauty
that has us mocking the jagged lines of fence posts, but straight and
                                                        climbing
then disappearing, there's symmetry and some are satisfied with this
                                                        regularity
as variation over the polished undulations . . . so, cutting to the
                                                        chase . . .
you asked about the crop-duster, the toss-about mosquito vehicle
that whines at not-far-above head height, operates
out of a paddock beside the airfield
where the shire has little or no jurisdiction?
Depraved . . . a little. (I'll show you my letter
to the paper . . . later.) It's yellow, with straight wings below the
                                                        fuselage,

below the cockpit—a sort of commonsense placement,
so the spray nozzles don't drop it over the pilot . . . proudly, their
                                                                advocacy
organisation calls them skilled avoiding loss through windshear,
hot on their GPS with variations, none of this old method
of kids running round paddocks with flags to guide
them in, atomising over their sconces; the one that cavorts
and despoils around here is not a turbo, but a piston-job, I'd guess,
highly—even radically—manoeuvrable—relatively
cheap to maintain . . . a mono-plane taking off from where
the old Tiger Moths did their tricks, this zipping
in and out, routing funguses and beetles; you mention
North by Northwest, well how about driving home along the
                                                        Spencer's Brook-
York Road and having a plimsoll line cut across your windscreen
as the yellow Mosquito swoops from paddock to paddock,
a cycling hallucination that has your sight severed into blue sky,
yellow knife, and a chemical fog, a re-jigged Goethe's *Faust* for the
                                                                wheatbelt—
the angles might be wrong, and the chasing lateral, but the driller
                                                                    killer
bloodbath cultism is clear enough . . . in a place where angles are
                                                                    relief
its sharp distraction from its cajoling smooth parabolas of descent,
are agnosticism in its blind faith: a jerking correction, a jagging
off the flight-line, betrays . . . anyway, here's my letter
to the newspaper: herbicide and poison spraying
is rampant everywhere, but York is a disturbing case-study.
Sometimes we have three different people spraying
the same patch of ground. At this very moment
our house is basically being dive-bombed by a crop duster
(it passes over on its way to paddocks down the road—
very very low)—this stuff is done right up to the town limits.
Some here think that it has brought major health problems
and even behavioural problems at the local school

(though I am sure the school would deny it — but this
comes straight from various teachers over the years). We've
had a neighbour decide he'd spray roundup
and SpraySeed twenty feet inside our (organic) property
boundary because he thought it was a good thing to do.
I have a million stories like this — including
the one where out at a famous old property
a friend of mine (an artist) was waving his hands
"telling" a crop duster to take a hike
when the plane took aim and literally
crop-dusted him — I am sure he can be reached
for a quote (he has since left York!). The boutique
town of horrors. It really is a catastrophe. Link
that with the unbridled aviation in the district
(it is selling itself as a place of leisure aviation),
and there's a disaster waiting to happen — we have,
often simultaneously, skydivers, small aircraft, ultra-lights,
hang gliders, gliders, crop dusters, and high-flying
commercial aircraft over York. I have spoken
with aviation authorities and even the health dept
over the years — all recognise issues,
but none can do anything about it. Post 9–11
the aircraft industry was supposed to be more regulated —
not in York. It's a cowboy scenario . . . I watched them fuelling
and taking on spray a few days ago . . . strange, this struggle towards
                                                    permanence,
where building-permit dead zones become layerings of growth and
                                                    poison . . .
the spray plane facing the road, head up, tail down, prop turning
slowly
as it was fed through at least two orifices — now, this is phantom
                                                    body,
this is the ectoplasmic vacuum dangerously hungry, the small men
feeding it smaller by halves, and enslaved . . . they might be pointing
to the black-shouldered kite hovering over the runway,

they might be creating bonds that stretch over years — this pilot,
his refueller, the farmer with his booty of poison — they might
be discussing the silence above the sound of the engine noise,
the amendments cast by unfurling shadows in the swoop,
the angular graphics, scrolling imprint that wears or washes off
instantly, a ploy, a counteraction of the spray's residualism . . .
I organise your wilderness the pilot thinks,
with gradual variation? Or full of altruistic sky-glean,
he plays the prophet, the comrade of Spitfire pilots
in the Battle of Britain, the battle these farmers
in the Avon Valley still imagine, fight, track
out of the Old Country's . . . bumpy weather,
not-nearly-perfect flying
conditions, waiting
for their dragonfly
to take the tree-huggers
in the Valley head-on,
incising their precious airspace,
their sky-is-falling complexes,
their lily-livered "allergenic" children,
the angularity of their spineless organic gardens,
their devils, their angels, their atheisms.

Beauty in Colour

Dampiera:
overtly blue;
kwongan's issue:
perennial's

annual show: sand
corridor, scrawls
colour and palls:
electric storms.

The space between
thin shadow forms
glabrous leaves, looms
out to asphalt

vegetation.

Deluge (cant) / The Eye

Instantaneous and not seeing.
                              A torrent
in the aqueous humour. A shindig of light
and graven images.
            What gaze owned by fixation
                    on gauze covering,
through a black veil the white moons shifting
as caught out, makes apprehension?
                              Though purple-black,
                    clouds violent above the house on the crest
        of the hill: bloating, restive in its cradle.
Drenched, there are no nerve endings
            to carry sound,
                    to elongate
        dramatic weather conditions,
the nation's "top scientist", slipping
back into the mining industry
            from whence he came;
                                    impact
                    mushrooms
            and enwraps, no needlepoint,
        whiling
away of evenings, candlelight
barely enough, to burn through
and coat the skin warm with friction,
suddenly cold when floodwaters
puddle
            around your feet;
                    drought keeps hocking
its old goods in the narrowing catchment,
                    drought is sodden fleece
trailing out ribcage, resolved internal organs: the wick

tapping barometer, nostalgia
            of fellow sheep — living — bracketed
around a powderbark, edge of gathered materials —
the reserve — agitate appendix and appendices,
      bodily opening out,
            worth capturing
a moment the mind clears, thinking
      dynamic: downpour has stopped,
            hemi-commandment
      has us cowering
            beneath white-tailed cockatoos
      further
north-east than we'd imagine (pro bono storms
that mantle, and still to come), no fear,
no quota,
            no restorative qualities of faith
gone up with the deluge,
                  going under?

Ugliness — A Vision

The terror of road-widening
to lessen the death toll, tricks
of the developer popping up like the exquisite
sense of losing control as you round the corner:
a high-risk accidental manoeuvre you feel
like doing again,
      as if merycism is not a disorder
but a joy — a chewing the cud of beauty,
the way something goes in and is forced out
with explosive sensation —
    going from loose gravel
to sand after torrential rain,
       sown fields weltering
and saying we'll crisp harder
         when drought reconstitutes,
ninety degrees at the crossroads
bowing out to one hundred
then one hundred and five
and the back end
pushing
    the heart into the mouth,
processing the angles
    and circumferences of correction,
       knowing what's left in the keel-hauling
of "land" is the celebration
purely on the level
of the single cell,
    behest of protoplasm,
       an argument or irritation
shifting response that deadly degree,
    the arc of a kite exquisite,
frankly beautiful;

so, what's made of a bricolage
         of death, sex, compound fractures
of vision and selfishness?
         Of the ascetic's prayer-
incantation
         when sleep comes down, shut-eyed
                  screen of collision,
the unseemly tree warped by high winds,
fire, the brutality of axes and children — maybe *you*
thirty or so years earlier —
                  bush-bashing
         the road's edge like a cult, crossroads
                  its vaticinal emblem —
in *that* corner of bush we trapped . . .
         and checked the traps cold at daylight,
macarised blood on teeth as ugly as . . .
         and souveniring a rabbit's foot
                  to empower in a split second
city-school emasculations,
         so smooth if stroked
the right way, though pressed hard
the bone disturbing the insides
of touch, prospects of luck;
                  widening
the road, they celebrate safety,
         tap down less deeply,
                  level rabbit warrens
with split levels, rectitude, consistency.

ESP in the Wheatbelt

Seasonal as once their coming here
was loss or bliss or change of scenery,
such draperies or oil on foundered iron,
pot shots at dawn, or prayers
said in pepper trees or halfway
down a well, or the glass
wandering across the board, names
spelt out through fog, twitching
branches of gravel-pit fires,
wash-away paddocks a semi-landslide
on gentle slopes, yet carrying
enough "externalisation of the senses"
to make palaver of the emotions;
cross-country she cried in recesses,
beneath sole trees in cleared spaces,
among stepped bricks of broken
and robbed houses, seeing nothing,
hearing nothing, tasting nothing,
smelling nothing, feeling nothing,
and yet the rush of dirt and blood
and the mercury dropping
below horizons, crowding
off lost or fading relatives,
hurt and pleasured and enlivened
runs and furrows, the wet 'n' dry
of a contra-spectrum, disk plough
scoring black out of white quartz agglomerations,
sub-currents sprung up like whispering
circuit boards, a wattle and daub
of storylines as resonant
as the hot kitchen, ink welling
out of the cracks in the bureau.

Textures of the Wheatbelt

Hessian waterbag cool in shade-house
swings with resistance, a cooling action
of flow that would slow flight down,
interfere with logic, a textural
draught, a rough divvying up of cloth
and air and water tilted against a burnished horizon,
stems of Paterson's Curse inflicting glass needles
like beacons, to rub against the angle of entry
like cropping out of season, or setting
a rabbit-trap off with a bare foot or sandal;
the shed strips of rough grey outer bark
of the York gum tune the green-grey
glide of undercurrents, the underneaths
out of sun and weathering winds,
gripping barbed wire to pin it down
and climb over to catch the flickback and skin-jag
and to wonder why you deserve such ill luck:
it's a matter of physics; an exfoliation of rust
is sharp and withering, crumbling cut,
all damage in bind-a-twine ripping over skin,
through clenched hands as bale slips sideways
and spills in segments, a burning as fire
and satin and density of colour,
red welts rising against the pliers' cut,
so much plant fibre and wire, blood slicks
like oil and water mixed against chemistry,
a science of bone finery and sharpness,
sinew and sever, a feathery drift of ash
made ash again where fires are burnt often,
where steel is extreme even through gloves,
and a clod of loamy earth sticks just right,
too much in heavy clay, too little in sand

welling out vast planes, low scrub gone,
a white scrunch echoing rims of brackish water,
wings and carapaces irritant and emollient
on harvest windscreens, grain-dust working
pores best described as agnostic
in their receipt of itch.

Sounds of the Wheatbelt

The grasshopper roar is almost the locust roar
though not quite a swarming, just holding off
an issue of damp and dry, though intensity
of insect traffic as three-dimensionally tense
the eardrum of the paddock strains and a barking dog
is hoarse against the rustling electric scrum,
the whirr, the racket, the scratching and clicking,
attempt to flip upright, rotoring hover, Doppler
rush-by, hell-diver and sound-barrier imploder,
scissoring and slicing, smashing and crunching,
serrations pulling and parting, riffling carapaces
to expose the sound-makings, staccato
premonitions, signalling nightfall and drawn-to-lights,
heat seekers and seers of the heart's glowing beating outline,
unearthing and gnashing out to pincer
the bull by the horns, flutter as fine as the wings
that reflect the eye of the wagtail, sun's stimulation . . . wing-walking
along hotlines of nymphs and egg-layings,
feathers see-sawing down from cracked dead branches
where an arguing and jesting flock of galahs high-balls
into sunset, zips ripped down and jamming skin,
crows beak-twisting and drawing out the inevitable,
thick rustle of bobtail with just-enough acceleration
to get down below the flurry of wingsters,
incendiary consumers in a rush to get done,
such a short claim to our already accustomed ears . . .
threatening to conflagrate the crackling grasses.

The Tastes of the Wheatbelt

Of the tongue things eaten make more words
than words make food, but that's no reason
we should succumb . . . asked at the cut-out piss-up
the shearer says taste . . . here is beer and lanolin,
blood of the sheep I shear . . . the brief
action of fire on the flensed beast . . . By slow burning
wood stoves, quick electric elements and blue gas jets,
the verdict is gravy and custard, salt and sugar,
and the ease with which a fork does or doesn't
prod the paddocks; taste is the most delusional
of senses, so many poisons sweet or inoffensive
to these multitudinous guardians of the temple
pass through undetected, so many sour tastes
prevent the absorption of essential nutrients;
dirt in mouth, toothpaste, tobacco . . . and kerosene
from the back of the hand wiped across the lips
without thinking . . . sampled "new foods"
ancient as bland tofu enlivened by soy sauce,
"old foods" as vibrant as wild jams and seed flours,
entrepreneurial cross-pollination
of the palate and erogenous zones,
the essence of home-baked bread—
wishful thinking against bad seasons,
rainwater stored in corrugated tanks
sweetly bitter with its taint of the metallic,
paradoxes of foods stained by woodsmoke,
taste of our own sweat, cauterised longing
brought by thirst, a blank zone induced
by scalding coffee, clove oil for the toothache
too far to drive to get it seen to, parrot-torn
stone-fruit a display of prepositions as the cyanide
of the bite-down releases stickiness

and a freshness beyond the mint
held in the cheek, tractor winging it
as the wheel spins below the ball
of the hand, dust become grit
and the concreting over of buds,
a dull bridging of the salacious creeks,
salt hardening the arteries, tasting
from this far apart: bitter almonds
breathed in through the mouth.

Smells of the Wheatbelt

Yes, the smell of hay being cut when slightly damp,
that heady, intoxicating lushness, a poison
sustaining allergies and full heads; yes, the wheat
harvest, the dry stalks cut and eaten by the header,
spilled like alcohol into the field bins, trucks
overloaded for the silos — both sides of a simile;
yes, the smell of wet sheep on a frosty morning
warming rapidly, the sun blazing though far
enough away to keep the temperatures down,
the olfactories unsure as stung and bitten; the sweet
putrefaction of a field of flowering canola, the weird
anomaly of wattle bloom, the layering of dust occluding
its own mineral and cellular odour; the perfumed
corrosion of herbicides killing from the roots up,
leaf down, inside out; sting of pesticides washed
from crop to river, the chromatic gleam
filming the surface a collusion of smell and taste,
a trauma of the eye the balancing liquid
plethoric, yellow patches of cells so close to seeing
the plumes and clouds of fumes, the effusors asnomiac;
the dog having rolled in the realm of the dead,
a secret place of dumped animals, ribs
splayed and skin hanging in coagulate "high heaven"
misrepresentation; in from labouring
over fencing, the underarm scouring
of shower and clean clothes: hedonic,
fugitive, diffuse, abated.

Clearing of Beauty

In the chopping-down then burning-off then picking-up
zeitgeist of the wheatbelt,
                    the lauding of fires
smouldering at twilight into the night,
                            the minor celebration
of the Albanian clearing team's strength
and modesty
            — posing for an axe-shot;
                                    some parts
were reached where indigenous people
would not go,
                where no land rights
are claimed,
            where it's bad territory
        and the land is poison
despite the abundance of flora and fauna,
            sparkling variety
        in low rainfall area,
                        run-off
from granite fuelling fifty-foot-tall she-oak
rain forests;
        going there unknowing
            is no excuse
to enter the taboo cave — so horrifying
        the legend that you depart with
                    is a sickness of knowing,
        wondering why it is a cold enters your head
                and your sinuses bleed,
                                where un-naming
won't remove the taint
                as the town harvests
        that run-off,

87

                    guiding it into their dam
to supplement the water supply,
                    but so majestic the humps
                              rising up out of the flat wheat-growing zone,
rock meadows pricking with trigger plants,
                                        a supersaturated
life of scrub and birds,
                    to surmount paramount top scale
and pinnacle
          the eroded forehead, busted skull
and exfoliated scarring;
                         to azimuth is to scan horizon
and encompass,
          to see the massive wedge-tail eagle sluice
upwards and
          — at eye level —
                              search
                    with its pivoting head,
          gyroscopic predation, to lie back
and let it sit in the air
          just above you,
                         so high up anyway,
                                        to say
no other species-crossover could be more intense
than the bone structures of such wings seen from below,
as emblematical
          as spiritual rights anywhere
at any time in the world,
                    counting five or six fully-flexed feathers
at the tips of the wings,
                         the seven across its tail —
fingers sensing you —
                    stroking / testing
more violently than talons,
more violently than a hooked-cutlassed beak:

            its weapons
are its feathers,
            its guidance system,
its eyes,
            its consciousness
of your tentative indulgence
                              of a moment's
crossing-over that can't ever happen,
                                        a sickness
that will rise up on you when you wake,
            start from brief sleep,
                              wondering
why you've been
                  where you've been,
            where the sublime is minuscule —
the beautiful vast thought
                        of elsewhere.

PART IV

Association (Sublime/Beauty): I drove on, a ghost . . .

Today . . . on the same stretch of road . . .
I listened calmly to AC/DC's *Highway to Hell*,
white gums equivocal in smoke pall
blanketing the district — a kind of amber-red lethargy
making reactions slow;
                         at the point of the promised land,
wondering about the exact meaning of the lyrics,
                                              I went
into old history, an associative history of the moment
and found no terror, as I hadn't when I'd died there,
on that bend,
              yesterday . . .
                         around 10.45 a.m.
The side-swipe of a truck travelling at no doubt
twice the speed limit —
                         the vacuum and ejection,
my spin-out on gravel shoulder,
                              careening
into a stand of white gums
              with enough growth to stand rigid
and preserved
              against the impact you brace yourself for,
                    in a reaction time like the time
                    it takes to catch a ball
batted at devastatingly high speed;
                              that I drove on,
a ghost,
         on roughly as if the truck
hadn't been there,
              hadn't destroyed my life and the lives of those close to me.
My death didn't bring assurance of afterlife
or respite

but rather life as life had always been.
All the trees in the same place,
more approaching traffic,
people celebrating or being lamented
on the radio you switch over to;
you just can't tell you're dead,
unless the certainty to the death-event is so overwhelming
it takes you back to the place of ending
to look over the evidence:
evidence which is just
not there.
Empty air and unmoved trees and Port Lincoln parrots
too far south, too far into a death zone
most disturbingly not a "parallel universe"
kind-of-thing: people
are *still* real or *unreal*, respond with agency,
and yet: I am dead, have died —
felt the moment
of passing, of being snuffed out, obliterated . . .
loss of uncertainty upending the promised land,
intelligently designed paradise,
the world left "behind" refilled
with the fleshed-out dead,
answering questions of loss:
don't
start over
dead
clearing the forests,
eroding the soil,
making extinct animals truly extinct —
here in my dead life, which is no more than my live one,
doing the "right thing" in too many small ways,
hoping for the cumulative . . .
I am thinking on the run here,
getting used to it.

The laws that remain,
the new laws I can't get around.
Deadlines to meet.
        A drive home at twilight
                'roos out on the road
a full moon ready
to drag out the dusk.

Fear

Green pools stranded by the sun's blank harshness,
Sky's indigo, stained glass of a hurricane lamp,
Distant fires coating the surfaces,
Sheep wired out of the river beginning to stamp.

Insects igniting in their tropospheres,
Whirligigs and diver beetles deprived of oxygen,
We sat on the bank harvesting our fears,
A car up on the gravel road revving its engine.

An oily-winged water bird anxiously perched
On the vitrified wing of an 'old-man' flooded gum,
Lurched as suddenly out over water and plunged,
We grew calm as it stayed down, caught at the bottom.

Transfixed, all sound ran as one, the world
Moved round too fast to calm;
Our fear bled dry as the paddocks whirled,
And we fed our love to the imagined harm.

Riding the Cobra at the York Show
(The Artificial Infinite)

Hoodwinked by the flat-lining, inside out
Silver lining of every absent cloud,
A clear day halo, a vulcanised rout
Of dust and eucalypt, diesels and loud
Stereos hyping up an eager crowd:
Addendum to truck and trailer, it rears
Up and contorts, hydraulically proud,
Eyes in the back of the head, cobra peers
Out into the hills and paddocks: it fears

Less with each scream. Down there — about to wake —
Snakes that wouldn't recognise it — dugites,
Gwarders, pythons, blind snakes . . . this clap-trap take-
All-before-it blow-in whiplash that skites
Loud enough to wake the dead, deny rites
Of belonging. Still, it rouses the prey
To come out into the open, reach heights
Once unimaginable; praise this lay
Society, almost too proud to pray.

Hooked elbow, steel lap-trap, drop-pod lock-down . . .
Centrifuge of senses and kinetics,
On the blow-out, rise up and twist, your frown
Looking down and out at the granite quirks
Of sunset ridges, peripatetics
Of ripening crops, glib orality
Of sideshow clowns, unravelling antics
Of object and shade . . . the finality
Of bent guns in shooting tents, reality

Sublimated and betrayed like roos caught
In a spotlight; centre of tension, soul
Lolling out of the mouth, memory fraught
With unresolved theologies, the roll
Of light and unction dipped in the blurred bowl
Of endolymph, the body osmotic;
This sharp arabesque as elemental
As Hyperion's car freaking parrots
And judges of the show's best: despotic!

So cedillas hanging heavy with bi-
Lateral agreement, torque and sentience
Weighed up in slowing, operator's wry
Perving as limbs unfold, his dependence
On post-rush joy hidden by a grimace:
Vertigo, obtuse valley-lift anchored
By hill's reprise. . . . cobra lodged in conscience,
Iron-clad alibi, convalescing, coiled
Double helix, lime-lit, reloaded — bored.

Terrible Darkness (Against the Racism of the Sublime)

There is no moon and the shock of black
anneals windows, faint reflection of darkened
room I emanate:
                "the idea of light in the eye"
strains the damaged outlines, species lost
like morning fog:
                it is dead centred night
and another cold front has torn past,
and the crossroads I'm sure are a whirlpool,
a vortex — will I look in daylight?

The conservative commentator
              interviewed from Washington
on SBS Australia,
              says looking at New Orleans
after Hurricane Katrina
                  is like looking at disaster
              in Haiti or the Ivory Coast:
I guess this is a criticism
              of white wealth, generic white
ability to escape the city
                  before its "saucepan"
filled with toxic sludge
              suspended in water,
but he can't see
              how racist it is in itself,
                  in all directions, insulting
to all *referents*.
              Not in the sludge,
his wisdom is the child
              suddenly given sight
                  and being terrified

by blackness alone,
                    his whitened blackness,
in itself:
            as if no other conversations
had come through darkness
                    I look out into, feasting
on my own luminous reflection,
eye muscles
            straining as darkness
    is pain,
as darkness taunts my
                    minus five diopter glasses:
I like darkness,
        I like the blackness between objects,
the blackness of objects,
                    reflecting
more than you think,
                the mopoke's
undulating call through to the first hint
of illumination;
                laden with grotesqueries,
we settle to watching and discoursing
the blind folly of nature walks;
                        the pain
        of the eye opened
full tilt in the space filled
        with long faded afterimages,
chemical bonfires of guilt or disturbance,
                            darkness
colouring the vortices,
                the old phase and amplitude
of sensing something is there,
            something you're about to trip over:
                roll of fencing wire, axe,
            wheel snapped from a trailer

laden with fallen limbs of salmon gum,
                              wandoo;
in New Orleans
          the housing behind the cemetery
                    is sold off with a pre-Civil-Rights determinism
          as a gravitational "black hole",
a sink of dark matter,
                    a missing mass
against which the police
shelter —
          is it for me to have an opinion
on this in the dark country of my room,
                              in the shade
of the "richest country
                    shockingly
needing help" as well? Surely,
          in the dark,
you help out,
          a hand guiding you
to the fence-line,
                    late back from furthest paddocks,
stumbling
          over quartz chunks
     barely remembered
beyond their white glitter,
                              their fools'-gold grin
of blasting sunlight;
                    to some, my skin
is dark enough to be "suspect" — grown up
calling ourselves "black Irish"
without knowing faintly why — apologists
are sure *it's* European in origin:
                              Portuguese sailors,
troops from the scattered
Spanish Armada?

I read *The Faerie Queen* by the glimmer
of an electric light
                 — sixty watts — in the next room,
the windowed door between — us — shut;
                                in teaching
physics in a darkened classroom —
                 experiments
involving optics and ripple tanks —
         the Nuffield Foundation suggests:
            "Shadows on the ceiling
     will reveal
              movements
         that are not
           in your
direct line of sight."
              In minimal light,
moths and gnats cluster about window frames,
       a shredded darkness, a soucriant
we look for, cultural backlash,
surprise attack.

Concerning Smallness: Golden Whistler

Exquisite song
Carries terror,
Default — error,
Utility.

Partner nearby.
Vicinity.
Movements scatty.
Black-shouldered kite

Pauses — deflected.
A singing rite
Vibrates the light —
Leaves glistening.

The range of song
Strains the awning,
Inverse praying,
Stretching of skin.

Listen — the non-
Newtonian
Liquid's resin
Shears away stress,

Elides duress.

A Place of Lichen

Grizzled on rocks and trees
a lukewarm green like a brand
of house-paint — a fad
long faded from the market; cladding
painted over, patios trained,
brought to order. A paint
that crackles with the heat,
peels and flakes with cold. Behaves
adversely in sunlight. A skin disorder,
a surface feint, epidermal quackery,
clustering about an area of wear:
elbow, knee, undercoat; the code
lost by its creator.

PART V

Some: an ode to the partitive article

Some burn-outs on asphalt stretch outside trig tables
Some galahs refuse to toe the line
Some solar cells gather waving lines of morphemes
Some striated pardalotes nidify just now, some shortly
Some spray booms disassociate, haze painted button quail
Some crop dusters plague the guy waving from his rooftop
Some bush bashers patiently tend some crops-in-the-bush you stay
        away from if you don't want to be shot
Some windmills shake down, rung on rung of saline accumulation
Some hubs on mallees mark driveways
Some samphire is salt bush in some necks of the clear-fell
Some wedgetail eagles harried by crows stay high above pasture
Some laterite conduits are County Peak
Some casuarinas are melaleucas are grevilleas are hakeas are acacias
                                                are
        eucalypts if you forget your guide book
Some poddy-dodgers are dodgers of law-makers and indulgers of
                               flesh in-takers
Some sandhi are a(n) handy way of vowelling a wheat harvester
Some intermediaries focus specific causes for a decline
        in yellow skink numbers
Some wattles hold back flowering (sometimes)
Some farmers drive past three times in case they've missed catching
                                    you
Some lives are lost on crossroads
Some parishioners visit other people's churches, temples, mosques . . .
Some internees collect, collate and work the earth — friends
        turn enemies, encryption of fences . . .
        offspring on town council
Some new migrants settle on marginal land, push scrub
        past breaking-point, fibro houses vacant now,
        companies taking profits

Some fettlers save money and send it back home, some drink it in the town
        saloon, rail now much diminished
Some kids at school say "foreigners" will knife you in your sleep—
        they marry the sisters of their enemies and have big families
Some kids sell tomatoes at roadside stalls, saying "buoni pomodori!"
Some prayers connect and others don't, all get played back,
        are held to account
Some red-capped robins rip into our dark spots
        and make light of them
Some polluted places are so beautiful
        they make you weep buckets . . .

Station Road and The Common Effects of
Poetry, Not by Raising Ideas of Things

Steel-blue of post-twilight, hard-edged here
on high ground with high clay content
      satisfying two requirements, salmon gum —
                              real salmon gum —
                        ridging
          and powerfully flexed,
recasting Station Road like shockwaves
           and vacant space written out, striking the rung
        past Uncle Jack's old place
             because of headlight dip, a loss in light
backlit by pencil-thin horizonal line of umber, sold off
               to Macherey,
        to those who'd plant Eastern States spotted gum
      on driveways or fencelines in the Western Provinces,
         a halcyon libertinism, as up at dawn
we undo evening light
        so invested, so declined in capitalism: on this drier ground
we'd fight sleep, to catch the tawny frogmouths,
                         to force down
through the well's dry wall,
             split sleepers tousling darkness:
"confiscation of the property of all emigrants and rebels"?
Aloneness in departure,
           mallee
a bounty out of reserve?

Off despotic inroads, a translator launches
      into trial crops, a flourish
of contaminants
      held out by tunnels of she-oaks cloistering
Station Road; lament the breaking up, the coming in, rejoindering

and fencing off, annexed tracks; *United by nature*, connecting
            the razzamatazz of soaks and dams, fences
                    down around flowering lucerne,
        the Needlings filled in again, blocked
against homestead and gunslits in white stone black;
it's a stepladder through speed reading
            driving so slow, the textual steps
of verandah lights welding outlines and tree forms
                    on edges both lost
definition,
        blended species, where a family chat
turns to the freaks and the fashionable:
                                didn't recognise
indentation of salt pan so late in life,
                        recomposed
        by dash-glow, odometer
and intensifying tail-lights
            a tricky way
                    through materialism's
compound aggregate.

Wet Wood

Wet wood — I am trying to light a fire
　　　　for warmth. In a few months
lighting a fire out here will be a crime —
　　　　a serious crime.
　　　　　　　Once,
when cooking on a Metters stove in summer,
　　　　spark-arresters, long chimney,
and a certain amount of luck played out
　　　　against total fire bans.

For cooking, you lit the fire before dawn,
　　　　or after sunset . . . hot baths
maybe once a week — a copper
　　　　heated on the stove top.
If a spark escaped and stayed illuminated
　　　　in its chaotic arc down
to bone-dry stubble, it'd all go up,
　　　　the house brought down
with paddocks, bush, roadside vegetation.
　　　　The fire would roll over gravel
and singe words of damnation and exasperation
　　　　spun out of neighbours' mouths.

So dry, there was no water to fight
　　　　fires with anyway.
You could retreat into the muddy slurry
　　　　of the house dam, and hope
you didn't succumb to smoke,
　　　　scorched air.
　　　　　　　Later,
when the mains power came through,
　　　　the risk of a spark

from the shed generator — 32 volts —
        was replaced by the risk
of powerlines whiplashing ignition
        in a high dry wind — 240 volts.

"We can't have war out here . . .",
        it was occasionally
argued . . ., "one explosion, one hot tracer,
        and we'd lose
everything . . ." So dry, it crackles
        with static, the blue flame
a "living nightmare" . . .

                  Wet wood —
I am trying to light a fire for warmth.
        In a few months
lighting a fire out here will be a crime —
        a serious crime.
While the wood is wet it's hard to spark
        a conflict. Though
we know how, how to burn
        the unburnable.

AN ADDITION

Into the Sun

The film of moisture on the eyeball sizzles
though it's not really hot outside: sun the other
side of gold and occasional cloud umber to gravitational black;
all surfaces are reflective from early morning rain,
and into the sunlight is bitter-sweet
and difficulty lifts from the asphalt; a twisted strip
of salmon gum bark laminate and the waste
from Blake's tree-angel — all angels excrete — has
you swerve away as if life depends upon curve
and intersecting line of shadow, long shade
permeating your semi-reflective exterior,
lull in crows' late life, startling your blind spot
navigating broken white line then double solid
strips of nuclear activity, eternal chain reaction
running aground past wooded cemetery, creeks leached
from Lover's Leap, a panorama of district occasionals,
keepsakes;
                I dreamt as you dreamt of a screen full of triangles
gone suddenly blank — seemingly in an instant, imagining
a flash though its opposite is incandescence sucked dry,
as sun visor is angled and head lifted above the straight
and narrow, roll of the downward slide, pryamoid or prismatic
slip from apex to base, a scrunching effect: that's what's left,
and I've no proof beyond an evening dullness, a late dusk
comparative: it's less harsh on the eyes but less
invigorating, less exposed to prayed for end result,
an aftermath left to keep the flocks
in order: so many cattle moving into sheep territory;
                                                    top-
dressing they use their spray pods, liquid fertiliser
like a coagulated mirage in cooler weather, seed-drilling
a sun-rippled pasture, a bearing taken

from the eye's corner, these indulgences
of a light so overloaded we'd never risk
staring it down if free choice
                            could change gravity
to a variety more sublime;
                            to the glint of immensity
in-foliate, like carbons in triplicate
when protogine, quick steps to levity.

Night Recall Station Road: typed in darkness

Walwalinj silhouette blown
sharp
      flooded gum overhang a blackly sparkling canker,
short-sheeted birdcall in damp,
                  like running the car slow
along Station Road to complete a second program, to rebus
and whorl the Cross Road unlocking, road driven
like an arched back under which all is hollow, the sound
of the cavernous even where the ground is low and saline,
she-oak huddle brushing silver magneto, sand and gravel dust
kicked out of the rain paste, yes, like water rushing, exhumation
of subterranean fractals, wheel ruts filled
with rocks, wagon flashbacks, axle
through thirteen separate land titles, striking
wrong keys like totems not belonging to you, knowing
after type is hot set there's no going back, harvester
still perched on rose quartz outcrop,
                tilted
away from the sun of pinpointing shadow
from fence to shaft,
          glow through sustain
plasticated Elders For Sale sign anaphoric
round boundaries, sober
post-restraint
        up to salmon gum canopy,
cavernous ride through cresting fallaways of ploughing
or straight-in seeding, no mucking around, stubble
misses like wire bristles so sharply upright, inevitable given
data to start with, no accidental imply or implore, well-water table
hillock osmotically stonewalled or inclined, thick in the throat
like spout or distended gullet,
           regurgitating, reflexing

sheep picking over red dirt first
green carpeting salutations against perfectly
stacked hay world, samphire offshoots so sharp
with finches still opposite thinning "rabbit bush",
Needlings backbone hanging there against gunshot, crossover
anatomies hoeing desiccated structure against rain,
in shed of pitch and tar, fire roll to circular breaks
a holding-off of paranoid potentials,
                                    slick
movements of nomadism, introduced weeds, burrs
carted across property on ignorant hobnailed boots
prised souls mis-striking wheat no-sprouted, lassitude of foliated
salt patch hard on all families, sure, but high on Station Road
they sell well at the expense of the low.

Stone Flung Near Head of Observer

The self-propelled mower guided along
firebreak regrowth, fresh growth,
growth sticking its head up too high,
to be lopped off, tall-poppied, struck
a blow for neatness and order, and so
out of Shire rules to prevent spread,
prevent the roll of fires, appease nervous
neighbours paring growth down to dust
on the dust of topsoil, tropes clouds
risen circumoral the blown to whole
face of summer, wind-roar of dustbowl,
and so the self-propelled mower
guided by the firm but gentle hand of a nice sort,
one city visitors might tantalise as "rustic",
replete with Yorkshire twists and compressions
of accent, though thirty-five years off the boat,
and so this observer mulling contrast
and balance, dizzying with revs per
thought and plenipotentiary nature
of cutters on brain-scan slice of planet,
thoughts of the solo quandong bristling
on the uncleared road, a thought of mortality
occurring much later, as brisk as a leaf's
point of breaking away, the first seized stone
shot past the lines of senses,
so close skin resounded around hair follicles
so close glancing down at spider in woodpile
so close the shed started like a nail gun
snapping into place, shed metal punctured
at angles and impact patterned as undoing
of forensics as the bullet that enters
and exits the fyke-style whole of imagination.

Prayer is loud, prayer is instant, prayer
lingers in anticipation, as sharp as the visuals
of stone flung close to head of observer
is blurred, distally connected to wherever
the bony centre of what's breakable
in the magnificent structure of our bodies
locates, spreads out largely and minutely.

A SECOND ADDITION

Forest Encomia of the South-West

Head State Forester, my grandfather
surveyed jarrah and counted pines
tucked into the hardwood
as soft sell, short shrift,
quick-growing
turnarounds; watched fire
sweep across his fiefdom,
crosscut into ledgers,
health of that jarrah and marri,
blackbutt on the fringe,
named the fastidiousness
of his Scottish wife
Ann Livy Plurabelle,
and made her Irish
where the convolution of sounds
was called "the bush", and dances
at Jarrahdale were as far
away as the hospital.

Kinsella is a road and a forest.
Kinsella is an overlay.
Kinsella is a post-war boom-time
verging on the changing ways.
He died when I was a few years old.
He smoked heavily.
Was tall with a parched face.
My father took me to look at the absent signifier,
the hollow birth-right. The fire-tower,
the ever-ready batteries' cardboard cylinders
still below, the phone smashed by vandals.

Up the fire trail, on the granite summit,
hard-core partying place.
Arsonist incidentals' irony
too good to refuse as the lighter gloats
in high temperature and fuck, man, you've set it off,
can't stamp it out, let's get the fuck out of here.
They don't say a word, ever. But you've
met them in pubs. You've seen the spark
in their eyes, their hatred of forests.

The resinous hardwood I split with an axe
as if under the seared surface
it's seamed;
                    from a young age the off-cuts
of his bush upbringing — my father, his father —
where he chopped the finger
off a cousin — a dare on the chopping block —
my father. His father walloped him.

The family from County Wicklow,
foresters there,
foresters here,
a man's man . . .
and you're Claude's
grandson?
Surprising.

2

Reportage? When
they came in at Ludlow
they cut the massive open-forest tuarts
and tried farming. That's the 1850s
and there's little talk
of Nyungar people in the forest,

though an artist tells me
there are Kinsellas who are blackfellas,
and I wonder why I've never met them,
heard of them. I want to find them,
for them to find me.

The sand-mining company
has the government in its pocket — this
is a barely renovated cliché —
and in the forest, police,
saying they'd be over the line
along with the dreadlocks and guitars
if the law told them to,
said all you can do
is watch the survey markers.
I ring lawyers. If they go outside
the allotted space . . . indigenous rights,
rare species, all are collated
in the effort to resist. Failure
allots expediency to the roadside camp
and issues of masculinity: locked on,
boys score points and tally arrests,
the forests goes under, girls
in dungarees call on the moon goddess,
and they move on.

3

My father, long separated from the forests
of his birth, drives through the wooded country
just for the sake of driving. I like to go up
into the hills, he says. Just to drive.

4

Surrounded by the paraphernalia of foresting
the cutting and tearing of bark is head over shoulder
in the pit, raining down flaky tears,
an electric rip — of the tongue,
taste not so unlike the taste we have of ourselves,
skin, flesh, chapels in a clearing,
wound sucked dry,
ice-skimmed water baptismally broken,
threads of mist as sunrises and sunsets
suffused are as much as we witness
on open plains, oceans;
never mind the pain
of working bullocks.

5

Giving the finger to a logging truck
is giving the finger to small-town rage
against heritage imagined as consistency
and moral equilibrium, as connection,
as vacant spaces grind logic into woodchips
and the spout shoots out time sheets.

Giving the finger to a logging truck
is to make the barrelled weight of trunks shift
against the squared U-prongs of praise, offerings-up,
gimleted throats to chain and separate
from the better halves of self; in the blood,
the rush is a drink in a bar that trucks no ferals.

Giving the finger to a logging truck
is a shooting offence, and a get-busted for dope-
carrying offence, and a laying-open of the secret

places retribution comeback getting ahead
making a buck fuck the old-growth lock-up
pent-up release, the swerve of the big wheel

ratio to asphalt and hitch-hiker
stranger danger fallout.

6

Mettle and impulse are group settlement
nano-probe Borg cube homesteads
rendering karri stands fused with paper
the good word is printed on,
anaphora in keeping accounts.
so lengthy the cordage,
building the State,
O liberty looked out upon
from the tall trees.

7

Sustainable equals dispossession.
Sustainable equals clear-felling.
Sustainable equals selective picking out of infrastructure.
Sustainable equals dieback.
Sustainable equals balance of payments.
Sustainable equals nice floorboards in parliamentary metonymics.
      Go where you want with this.
Sustainable equals God at the top of the pyramid, logging companies
                        the next rung down.
Sustainable equals the wood for the trees.
Sustainable equals the log in your eye, the splinter in your sister's.
Sustainable equals ochre rivers and a peeling-back of the layers
      of allegory — extended metaphors all the way to the sea.

Sustainable equals the widened highway and its support services'
                                                    flow-on effect.
Sustainable equals the commiserating blocks on the forest's edge
                                                    reaching
    into the forest bit by bit with the environmentally-minded
                                                    eroding their
    privilege bit by bit.
Sustainable equals the forest-loving dope-grower who crushes the
                                                    micro with every step,
    as delicate and caring as they might be, introducing weeds as
                                                    s/he
    never would with prickly pear or rose, the rabbits loving
    the tender shoots, O children of nature.
Sustainable equals dieback trod and trod through by effusing
                                                    bushwalkers
    infiltrated by bird calls — shocked into spirituality by the
                                                    weather calls
    of white-tailed black cockatoos.
Sustainable equals stars cut out around milling towns, forming the
                                                    southern cross
    in nation-building recognition of later migrant influence.
Sustainable equals forest by any other name.
Sustainable equals election promises
    come up trumps, couched in reassurances.

8

It's so wet in there: wetter
than anywhere else. A deflected wet
that intensifies, gets under all cover.
In the ice cold you sweat,
and are we under the layers,
the canopy focusing
hard-hitting echoes
on every pore,

clasping undergrowth
too succulent, luring
you in where it's no drier.

9

Extra-wide gravel roads
deep south so fire won't roll
as smoke so dense
you crawl
slower than through the worst fog
tightened windows preventing
the suffocating sting
you associate with those
you love most, love most
in the time left to you,
the pluming crown of flame
as much a vision
as you're going to get.

Acknowledgements

Poems in this collection have previously appeared in the following publications: *The Age*, *The Australian* ('Poets Paint Words'), *The Best Australian Poetry 2005*, *Daedalus*, *The Harvard Review*, *The Hudson Review*, *Live Poets Society 15th Anniversary Anthology*, *London Review of Books*, *New Welsh Review*, *Poetry Ireland*, *Poetry Review*, *Prairie Schooner*, *Raritan*, the *Reader*, *Smartish Pace*, *Southerly*, *Southwest Review*, *Times Literary Supplement*, *Turnrow*, *Watershed*, *West Branch*, *World Literature Today*.

"Sounds of the Wheatbelt" was awarded the Elizabeth Matchett Stover Memorial Award for best poem published in the *Southwest Review* in 2005. "A Place of Lichen" was part of a group of three poems by John Kinsella awarded the Annual Prairie Schooner Strousse Award for poetry (2005). "Forest Encomia of the South-West" was shortlisted for the Forward Prize (Best Poem of the Year), in the UK. "A Difficult First Harvest" includes a small amount of "found" text (astronomical).